"Who says accurate, cutting-edge science has to be a bore? Dembski and Witt make the biological nuts and bolts come alive and dance. They show that intelligent design is not only true, it's fun!"

Michael Behe, professor of biochemistry, Lehigh University, and author of *Darwin's Black Box*

"*Intelligent Design Uncensored* is a five-star fantastic voyage! Nonscientists will be swept up by the lively, readable story of discovery while aspiring young scientists will learn why their experimental work in the lab will do just fine without Neo-Darwinism telling them where to go."

Dr. Philip S. Skell, National Academy of Sciences, and Evan Pugh Professor Emeritus, Pennsylvania State University

"The book we've all been waiting for—a down-to-earth and clear explanation of the stunning scientific discoveries which underpin intelligent design theory and its implications, as well as a comprehensive rebuttal of the common objections. This book will excite the layman and provide a valuable starting point for the serious student of the science of origins."

Alastair Noble, Ph.D., chemistry, former BBC Education Officer and Her Majesty's Inspector of Schools for Science, Scotland

"Darwinians fired away throughout 2009, the 150th anniversary of *On the Origin of Species,* but could not kill the concept of intelligent design. This book is the first salvo of the next 150 years. Dembski and Witt succinctly explain what the war is about in a way understandable to a general audience. If people you know have bought the propaganda that ID is just a gussied-up version of six-day creationism, give them this book."

Dr. Marvin Olasky, editor-in-chief, *World,* and provost, The King's College, New York City

"Don't let its conversational, non-technical prose fool you; *Intelligent Design Uncensored* is a first-rate introduction to the intelligent design debate from two writers who know the subject better than just about anyone else. A useful resource for students of all ages!"

Guillermo Gonzalez, astrobiologist and coauthor of *The Privileged Planet*

"Dembski and Witt are the perfect combination. They deliver an explanation of intelligent design that is at once precise, lucid and, well, witty. *Intelligent Design Uncensored* shows that ID is not only intellectually serious, but intuitively compelling. ID is widely misunderstood and maligned by its critics, and sometimes hard to grasp, even by its friends. If you're wondering what all the fuss is about, read this book."

Jay Richards, coauthor of *The Privileged Planet* and author of *Money, Greed and God: Why Capitalism Is the Solution and Not the Problem*

"A tour de force in which two prodigious intellects apply their remarkable communication skills to the relentless pursuit of truth . . . and a sterling example of open-minded scientific inquiry that allows facts to lead wherever they may. Congratulations to Dembski and Witt for ably dismantling the stereotypical caricature of intelligent design."

Hank Hanegraaff, The Bible Answer Man and author of *Fatal Flaws: What Evolutionists Don't Want You to Know*

Intelligent Design

UNCENSORED

An Easy-to-Understand

Guide to the Controversy

William A. Dembski
& Jonathan Witt

IVP Books

An imprint of InterVarsity Press
Downers Grove, Illinois

InterVarsity Press
P.O. Box 1400, Downers Grove, IL 60515-1426
World Wide Web: www.ivpress.com
E-mail: email@ivpress.com

InterVarsity Press® *is the book-publishing division of InterVarsity Christian Fellowship/ USA*®, *a movement of students and faculty active on campus at hundreds of universities, colleges and schools of nursing in the United States of America, and a member movement of the International Fellowship of Evangelical Students. For information about local and regional activities, write Public Relations Dept., InterVarsity Christian Fellowship/USA, 6400 Schroeder Rd., P.O. Box 7895, Madison, WI 53707-7895, or visit the IVCF website at <www .intervarsity.org>.*

All Scripture quotations, unless otherwise indicated, are taken from the Holy Bible, New International Version®. NIV®. *Copyright* ©*1973, 1978, 1984 by International Bible Society. Used by permission of Zondervan Publishing House. All rights reserved.*

Interior Images: Artist's rendering of the Double Helix and the Bacterial Flagellum Motor: Used by permission of Illustra Media; Mount Rushmore: Barbara Harvey/BigStockPhoto; Grand Canyon: Courtesy of Elaina Whittenhall; U.S. Mint image: Wikimedia Commons; Crude arrowheads: Courtesy of Heather Reichstadt, curator of Charles D. Tandy Museum, Southwestern Baptist Theological Seminary; Weathered Burial Mounds: Georgy Markov/ BigStockPhoto; Hillside Mona Lisa: Used by permission of Barton Howe; Centriole from its proximal end and cross section of a single centriole: Used by permission of Jonathan Wells.

Design: Cindy Kiple

ISBN 978-0-8308-3742-7

Printed in the United States of America ∞

Library of Congress Cataloging-in-Publication Data

Dembski, William A., 1960-
  Intelligent design uncensored: an easy-to-understand guide to the
controversy / William A. Dembski and Jonathan Witt.
    p. cm.
  Includes bibliographical references and index.
  ISBN 978-0-8308-3742-7 (pbk.: alk. paper)
  1. Intelligent design (Teleology) 2. Evolution (Biology)—Religious
aspects—Christianity. I. Witt, Jonathan, 1966- II. Title.
BS659.D46 2010
231.7'652—dc22

                                                                      2010000917

P	21	20	19	18	17	16	15	14	13	12	11	10	9	8	7	6	5	4	3	2	1
Y	27	26	25	24	23	22	21	20	19	18	17	16	15	14	13	12	11	10			

Contents

1

Fantastic Voyage

DID MIND MAKE MATTER, or matter mind? Are the things of nature the product of mindless forces alone, or did creative reason play a role? Theologians have grappled with this question but so have philosophers and scientists stretching from ancient Athens to modern Nobel Prize winners like physicists Albert Einstein, Arno Penzias and George Smoot. The reason is simple: It may be the most important, the most fundamental question of all.

In 1859, British naturalist Charles Darwin introduced his theory of evolution to argue that blind nature had produced all the species of plants and animals around us. The new theory convinced a lot of people that evidence of a Creator could not be found in nature. If there were things in nature that remained mysterious, scientists would figure them out in time. To attribute its origin to God, they insisted, was simply to give up on the enterprise of science.

Today, Darwinists level the same charge against the contemporary theory of intelligent design (ID). They insist that ID is just an argument from ignorance—plugging God into the gaps of our current scientific understanding. Darwinists have made many thoughtful arguments over the years, but this isn't one of them. The theory of intelligent design holds that many things in nature carry a clear signature of design. The theory isn't based on what scientists don't know about nature but on what they do know. It's built on a host of scientific discoveries in everything from biology to astronomy, and some of them are very recent discoveries. To show what we mean, let's take a journey.

MIRACLE OF RARE DEVICE

Imagine you are a world-class software architect living twenty years in the future, and you just learned that you've won a lottery for a space flight to an unnamed distant planet. The rendezvous point for departure is the Jet Propulsion Laboratory in Pasadena, California. When you arrive, the scientists in the obligatory white lab coats seat you in a white conference room and explain that the flight will employ what they refer to as "mass driver technology"—no rockets, no flames and thus no need for an enormous launch pad. You'll depart directly from JPL.

After a thorough physical, you enter the raindrop-shaped vessel along with the captain, pilot and two other lottery winners. You're strapped into a cockpit seat in front of a panoramic viewing window and hooked to various wires, patches and tubes. On your left is a lottery winner with thick, hairy arms. He looks and talks like an aging steel worker from Pittsburgh, though you soon learn that he's actually a top-notch submarine engineer. The woman to your right is a gangly blond in her thirties, a Cal Tech physicist who keeps peppering the captain with questions about the mass driver.

The hatch is shut. The countdown begins. At seven you hear a low, groaning. At five it drops an octave and your teeth vibrate inside your gums. At three the lights flicker. At zero the cabin falls silent, a stab of pain runs the length of your body, and you fall into darkness.

When you wake, drooling, eyes blurry, head aching, you have no idea how long you've been asleep. A minute? An hour? A day? You rub your eyes and see that the ship is already approaching a moon or planet marked by a pattern of blobs haphazardly swinging this way and that over the surface. Maybe they're tornados, except that they're moving in all different directions. Would a storm do that? As the ship draws closer, you realize the moon isn't quite like anything from our solar system that you've ever heard about. The colors, the details are wrong somehow.

Noticing that you have the arms of your chair in a death grip, you try to relax. Farther and farther the ship descends. It's clear now that this strange moon is closer and smaller than you supposed, maybe only a dozen miles away and as many across.

If it's an asteroid, though, it's a strange one—almost perfectly round. You glance to either side to read the expressions of your fellow lottery winners. They're wearing the same blank look of wonder you are.

You turn back to the approaching moon, and here a curious thing happens. Though the moon had seemed small a moment ago, it now seems enormous again, not because you go back to thinking it's big for a moon but because you realize you're not approaching a moon, not a planet, but a machine of some kind, one far bigger than any manmade object you've ever met.

As your ship draws closer, you make out, across the thing's surface, millions of portholes opening and shutting as millions of ships enter and exit. A sensor beeps gently at the pilot's control panel. "I suggest the three of you breathe," he says, turning toward you with a smile.

You take a few deep breaths, but a moment later you're holding your breath again. You were expecting your ship to move into orbit around the space station, but now you realize that one hole—barely larger than the ship—lies directly ahead and the pilot is making straight for it.

You find yourself counting down from ten, wondering if these will be the final seconds of your life.

The engineer beside you crosses himself and murmurs, "What is it?"

"Byzantium," the captain answers mysteriously.

In the next moment you're through the portal and on the other side.

In modern parlance the ancient capital city of Byzantium, with its intricate and devious political environment has come to serve as a metaphor for all things labyrinthine and, well, Byzantine. Immediately you understand why the captain would refer to your destination by the name of that ancient city. Within is a realm of dizzying sophistication, a labyrinth of intricate corridors and conduits networking off in every direction, some stretching off to processing units and assembly stations, others to what the captain explains is an enormous computer, as yet far out of sight, at the center of the space station.

On and on you fly. When the central processing unit at last rounds into view, it looks like a space station itself, about a half a mile across and shaped like a geodesic dome. The pilot threads the ship through a tiny portal. Inside, in every direction you look, are mile on mile of spiraling staircases. "They're not for walking on," he says. "They're for storing data. They're part of the hard drive."

"I had no idea we were this advanced!" the lottery winner to your left says. "How did we manage it?"

"Us?" the pilot says. "Don't be silly. You have to realize, this factory does something human factories don't—it builds copies of itself. "

So it's even more sophisticated than you first imagined. You glance at the passenger to your left. She's biting her fingernails. Like you, she probably doesn't want to play the role of the theatrical passenger, doesn't want to voice the explanation hanging in the air—that this amazing space station must be the work of some alien civilization light years ahead of our own.

The pilot continues with his explanation. "Don't get me wrong. As extraordinary as this factory is, it isn't perfect. Occasionally when it builds a copy of itself, there's a minor difference, a copying error. But as the French say, *vive la différence.* Those tiny differences make all of this around us possible. You see, occasionally, one of those copying errors was actually an improvement. The improvement was preserved, and over time a series of these tiny improvements led to the extraordinary factory before us. Initially the factory was quite crude, but over time . . ."

The woman beside you—the physicist—interrupts. "How crude could it have been if it could build copies of itself? We've never managed to build a factory that could build a factory that could build a factory that could build a . . ."

"What are you suggesting?" the pilot snaps. "Are you some sort of religious freak?"

The physicist blinks, disoriented by the seemingly random charge. "No, I . . ." She tries again. "I just mean that the engineers who built this must have been brilliant. It's phenomenal."

The pilot's indignity falls away and is replaced by an expression of one amused and relieved by a sudden realization. "I think we have a little misunderstanding. Do you three have any idea where you are?"

"No, nobody's told us," the physicist says.

Here the captain cuts in. "Everything was on a need-to-know basis. You three were chosen each for a particular expertise—an engineer, a physicist and a software architect. The entire project is on the qt. Very hush-hush."

As you listen to this strange conversation unfold, you realize that the spiral staircases outside the panoramic viewing window seem to have grown larger. The ship has drawn up beside one, and it occurs to you that the staircase or ladder seems oddly familiar. Like the others, it has a pair of spiraling rails running parallel and joined across the middle by . . . Suddenly it hits you, but the engineer beside you speaks first. "A DNA model—the size of a building!" He tries to leap from his seat to point, but he's caught by the intricate restraint system. "Look! The intertwining rails are the double helical structure, and notice they're joined across the middle by the nitrogen bases. It's all coming back to me."

"*Nitrogenous* bases," the pilot corrects him, gesturing for him to stay put. "Adenine, thymine, guanine and cytosine."

"The genetic code's four-character alphabet," says the captain. "A, T, G and C for short."

"This is where genetic defects come from," the pilot adds. "Cystic fibrosis, Down Syndrome. If there's a genetic defect, eventually you'll find a glitch in a strand of DNA."

You recognize the four bases now, the four letters, by the way the adenine fits like a puzzle piece to the thymine and the guanine to the cytosine. This and the architecture of the double helix are the essence of order, of regularity.

However, as you study it more closely, you see that not everything about it is regular. The sequence of letters on any given rail follow one another in a seemingly random pattern.

The engineer interrupts your train of thought. "If this models DNA, what's all of this other . . . the space station, I mean."

"The larger sphere is the cell as a whole," the pilot says, "and the smaller inner sphere is the nucleus—where the biological information is processed and shipped out as code for helping build the various protein machines," the captain adds.

You and your fellow passengers are trying to process several things at once. Does this really model one-celled organisms? Could a tiny cell really be this sophisticated? And is it possible that the most ambitious government program could build such an elaborate model on such an enormous scale?

The engineer beside you breaks in with another question. "If the United States—planet Earth, humans, whatever—built this model, this space station, why was I brought in? My engineering work looks like tinker toys beside this stuff."

The captain takes a deep breath and proceeds to drop the other shoe. "Humans didn't build this. And, no, an extraterrestrial race didn't build it either."

"Nobody built it," the pilot interjects.

The captain continues. "You know how physicists have been trying for the better part of a century to unite Einstein's theory of relativity with quantum physics—the physics of large bodies with the physics of the subatomic realm? A couple years back, a pair of physicists at JPL finally succeeded."

"*The theory of everything*," the pilot adds.

"So-called," the captain continues. "This discovery has allowed us to make a series of technological breakthroughs more rapidly than anyone imagined. The details of those breakthroughs are still classified, but as we develop these new technologies, we have to recruit more and more talent to keep pushing forward. The three of you have been recruited into the project."

A new and rather disturbing explanation for their situation has begun to dawn on the lottery winners. At last the captain brings it out into the open. "The so-called 'theory of everything' has taught us how to miniaturize things," he says. "When you woke from the initial shock, the miniaturization process was well under way. That vague blob you saw when you first woke up? That's a cell, looking about as big as cells looked in the best microscopes of the nineteenth century. Those microscopes enlarged things about seven-hundredfold, and when you woke, you were seven hundred times smaller than normal, meaning the cell looked seven hundred times bigger. Then, as we drew closer to the cell, we continued to shrink down, down, down until we were a thousand million times smaller than our original size. This allowed us to enter the cell and then the cell nucleus.

"In the nineteenth century the cell was a black box, a mystery. Most scientists pictured the cell nucleus as relatively simple, like a little sack of goo. As you can see, they missed the mark. It's so intricate we're still trying to unravel it."

As the ship weaves its way through the nucleus over the next few hours, you witness a stunning array of raw materials and finished products shuttling along microtubule tracks to and from the many assembly plants in the outer regions of the larger and encompassing cell factory. It becomes apparent that the machines all around the ship are not only almost incalculably numerous but also fantastically various.[1] There are molecular machines to haul cargo along molecular tracks. There are molecular cables, molecular ropes, molecular pulleys. There are light-powered machines that harness particles of light and store them in molecular batteries, machines to flip cellular switches, machines to send electrical current through nerves, machines to build other machines (and themselves), machines to swim, machines to copy, machines to ingest and digest. In every direction you look, you discover some new miracle of rare device, nanotechnology light years beyond anything humans have yet achieved.

After a period of stunned silence, the engineer finds his voice. "How does the cell know how to build all of these machines, fuel them, orchestrate them?"

"It uses the same thing a computer uses," the captain says. "Information. Some of that information—not all of it—is stored on these winding staircases all around us, on the DNA—short for *deoxyribonucleic acid*. The DNA is like a software program, and its four-character alphabet—A, T, G and C—combine in various ways to form a twenty-character alphabet of amino acids. Each amino acid 'word' is three DNA letters long. Those twenty different amino-acid words are used to write the long protein sentences, the molecular machines you see working all around us."

Figure 1.1. Artist's rendering of the double helix

As a software programmer, you suddenly realize why the sequence of DNA letters didn't follow some regular pattern like ATGCATGCATGC . . . You realize why they're lined up in a nonrepetitive order. The physicist is thinking along the same track. "I get it now," she says. "I couldn't figure out why the As, Ts, Gs and Cs seemed to be stacked onto the double helix almost at random. But it's so obvious now. The order isn't random. They're coding information, genetic information. Novels and computer programs and instruction manuals—things like that don't use recurring patterns of letters. They couldn't convey their information that way. It would be like trying to write a friend where B always had to follow A, and the Cs had to come in threes. If every letter you set down was governed by a rule like 'repeat the letter and then skip ahead two letters in the alphabet,' you'd never get anything meaningful written."

The captain nods. "A postcard to a friend, a murder mystery, a software program, the DNA inside a cell—you name it, if you're going to code information, you can't be shackled at every step by predetermined laws. Now that doesn't mean you can set down the letters at random. Imagine going into a software program and randomly shuffling around the code. You'd crash it. The same thing happens when you start randomly shuffling around the letters down here. Last month we lost a crane operator when he started fiddling around with an amino acid sequence on one of the molecular machines. The machine crashed and took him and the crane ship down with it. The letters appear in a very specific sequence for a reason. That's the sequence that works for that particular machine."

"But random changes do occur in the order of the letters," the pilot adds, "and they're not always lethal. Sometimes they're helpful. That's evolution."

The captain rolls his eyes, and the two men fall into a heated debate that's hard to follow—something about whether individual mutations in the sequence of letters along the spine of the double helix (the sequence of As, Ts, Gs and Cs) can account for all of the sophisticated biological machinery around you. As they pilot their way from the cell nucleus and then from the cell, the debate grows so heated they almost run into a whiplike machine extending from the outside of a bacterial cell moving past the ship.

"Whoops!" the pilot says as he grabs the yoke at the last minute and steers around the spinning object.

"This little baby's called a bacterial flagellum," the captain says. "It's a rotary engine. Bacteria use them to get around. It has a proton motive force drive system, spins up to 100,000 rpm and can switch rotational direction in a quarter turn."

More of the whiplike flagella extend from the sides of the bacterial cell, and as you fall in behind it you see that it uses them in tandem as part of a sophisticated accelerating, braking and steering mechanism. As the ship approaches the nearest one, it's clear that the thing doesn't merely resemble an outboard motor. It *is* an outboard motor. There's the bushing with its L and P rings, a universal joint, the stator with its studs and C ring, the rotor with an M and S ring, even a drive shaft. As you descend on the whiplike propeller from above, the captain miniaturizes the ship some more and the pilot flies in for a closer look.

"The outboard motors we build can't repair themselves, but this one can," the captain explains. "It also harnesses the fluid it swims through for fuel. The way it does this is so complicated we couldn't unravel it till we were able to miniaturize ourselves and look at it up close. According to our pilot, this motor evolved from a much simpler version, one tiny mutation at a time. The

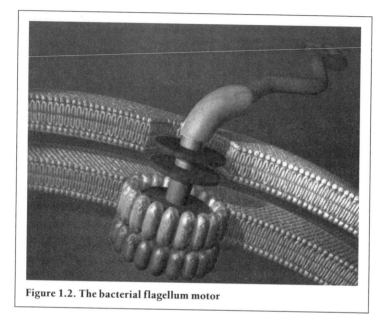

Figure 1.2. The bacterial flagellum motor

mutations had to be tiny because large mutations are always bad news. They either damage or kill."

The pilot nods. "It's a question of probabilities. A small positive mutation would, at least in theory, involve one or, at most, a very few random changes to a sequence of letters on a strand of DNA—the sequence of As, Ts, Gs and Cs along the spine of the spiral staircases we saw inside the cell. But a random mutation that produced a brand new kind of body part in one go would require hundreds and even thousands of DNA changes, all of them just so."

The captain adjusts an instrument and then rejoins the conversation. "It's sort of like dumping a box of Scrabble letters onto the playing board and finding that it just happened to spell out a superb and finished game of interlocking words. Darwin dismissed the idea of large-jump mutations. He was convinced they were beyond the reach of chance. Later experiments proved him right. If you're going to get to the promised land of a fully evolved flagellar motor, you have to do it one tiny mutation at a time. But there's a problem with that approach too. Darwin realized that nature eliminates defective mutations. If you bathe fruit flies in radiation, some of their offspring will be born with four wings instead of the usual two. They look cool. The problem is, they can't fly. Out in the wild they'd starve. Or get eaten. So they'd never have a chance to pass on their four-wing mutation to the next generation. And if by some freak chance one of them did, his poor kid would starve or get eaten."

The pilot tries to interrupt here, but the captain plows forward. "Natural selection is pitiless. It sifts out the crippled mutants that can't survive in the wild. This is why each mutant, from simple ancestor to finely tuned motor, has to be functional if progress up the evolutionary mountain is to continue. This isn't controversial. All of the biologists in the debate agree on this point. So, do you see the problem?"

"There is no problem," the pilot interjects, shaking his head in disbelief at the captain.

But the captain is also shaking his head. "No, I think there is. One biochemist explained it this way. The flagellar motor is like a mouse trap. It needs all of its parts to function. Take one part away from a mousetrap—say the spring—and you don't have a mediocre mousetrap. You have a collection of parts that is zero threat to a mouse. The bacterial flagellum's the same way. Take one of the protein parts away from this flagellar motor and you don't end up with a slower, clunkier motor. You end up with a pile of junk. And since the Darwinian mechanism can only build by seizing and passing on one *small, useful* variation at a time, it isn't a good candidate for building a machine like this. Each step in the evolutionary process has to be small enough to be handled by chance. And each step has to be functional or nature discards it. But with machines like the flagellar motor, only the *last* step in the construction process gives you a working motor. The evolutionary process needs a single giant leap forward, but Darwinian evolution doesn't do single giant leaps forward."

The pilot is getting impatient. "This biochemist you're in love with totally ignores the possibility of evolution co-opting machines from other systems along the way. They've even found a molecular machine, a little microsyringe, that could have served as a functional step on the way to the flagellum motor. How many other functional steps along the way have we just not discovered yet? Your biochemist's failure is the most embarrassing failure of all—a failure of the imagination. He can't stand to think that nature might be more creative than he is."

"Actually, he's addressed your co-option argument in detail," the captain says.

"His argument isn't even an argument *for* intelligent design," the pilot says. "It's just a negative argument against Darwinism."

"That's wishful thinking on your part," the captain persists. "He offers positive evidence for design. It runs like this: We know from experience that intelligent agents build intricate machines that need all of their parts to function, things like mousetraps and motors. And we know how they do it—by looking to a future goal and then purposefully assembling a set of parts until they're a working whole. Intelligent agents, in fact, are the one and only type of thing we have ever seen doing this sort of thing from scratch. In other words, our common experience provides positive evidence of only one kind of cause able to assemble such machines. It's not electricity. It's not magnetism.

It's not natural selection working on random variations. It's not any purely mindless cause. It's intelligence—the one and only."

"But that's not science!" the pilot exclaims, slamming his fist down on the console.

"Shouldn't someone be piloting the ship?" the physicist beside you pipes in meekly.

"Don't worry," the pilot tells her with a reassuring smile. "It's on autopilot."

This is good to know because the pilot and captain now plunge deeper into their argument. You close your eyes as the vessel slips through the turbulent wake of the flagellar motor's spinning filament.

Of course, the captain, pilot and voyage are make-believe, but the debate is real. As we will see in chapter three, it's taking place among contemporary scientists like biochemist Michael Behe and biologist Kenneth Miller, and has spilled onto the pages of the world's most prominent newspapers and science journals. The intricate world of the cell described in this chapter's story is also real, and the discovery of the world of this rare device drives the contemporary theory of intelligent design.

2

The Design Revolution

WE TOOK A MICROSCOPIC VIEW of life in the first chapter. Now let's step back and take in the panorama. The controversy over intelligent design is partly about how best to interpret a range of scientific evidence, but the controversy reaches beyond science because ID challenges an idea entrenched in the academic, legal and media establishments. The idea is called *philosophical materialism*. It holds that the material realm is all there is, ever was or ever will be. Philosophical materialism is the polite name for atheism. It's the billiard-ball view of reality: everything and everybody are really just so many particles knocking around in space, devoid of ultimate purpose. According to this view, things like courage, beauty, love, good and evil are illusions since, in the end, they can all be reduced to the interplay of matter and energy. Angst is really indigestion. Love is merely hormones.

Only about one in ten Americans is an out-and-out atheist, but atheists have managed to extend their influence by selling religious people a related idea called *methodological materialism*. In its most ambitious form, methodological materialism says that we can believe whatever we want in our personal life, but when we're doing serious academic work, we should only consider and defend explanations fully consistent with *philosophical materialism*. Otherwise, we might invoke the divine for things that later get explained by purely material forces—things like lightning or storms or romantic love. And wouldn't that be embarrassing, God getting squeezed out of the little gaps we stuffed him into? Better to play it safe by assuming that everything in the universe has some purely material cause—the origin of human language, the origin of life, the origin of the universe and so forth. Better to keep God tucked away, safely outside the universe.

By popularizing *methodological materialism* in this way, *philosophical materialists* have sought to render their academic opponents harmless. The idea has such a grip on academia that its most ardent proponents have been able to use it to demote, sue and even fire scholars who either made a design argument or mentioned intelligent design in the classroom.

Advocates of intelligent design have not been cowed. We're convinced that too much is at stake. Intellectual freedom is at stake. Instead, we're arguing in blogs, documentaries, university debates, books and academic articles that methodological materialism, far from furthering science, hinders the scientist's chief duty to follow the evidence where it leads.

WHAT DARWIN CHANGED

Ground zero in the controversy has been intelligent design's challenge to modern Darwinism. This is because Darwinism is the lynchpin of modern materialism.

In his 1859 book *On the Origin of Species*, Darwin argued that all life evolved from a common ancestor by purely blind material processes. Already before Darwin's theory, many believed that science had successfully explained almost everything in nature without recourse to a Creator. They even believed that the beginning of life—the origin of the first one-celled organism—was no big deal, since most biologists assumed these tiny cells were little more than glorified blobs of Jell-O. There was only one major branch of nature that seemed to hold out—the diverse, intricate world of plants and animals. These sophisticated living machines practically screamed design. They had even the most religiously skeptical scientists stumped. Darwin changed all that. He was the first to offer a plausible explanation for the diversity of life without invoking a Creator.

SURVIVAL OF THE LUCKIEST

Darwin's two-part mechanism is easy to grasp. First, when living things reproduce, they don't make identical copies of themselves. If they did, there could be no evolution. Every generation would be the same as the previous one. But offspring do differ from their parents. The biggest reason we're different from our parents is that we're a mix of their genes. But there's another reason for differences, one that usually involves tiny changes. These are the *random* variations that cause a lucky gorilla to be stronger than either parent, or a lucky gazelle to be smarter than his savvy mother and faster than his speedy father (or in the case of an unlucky gazelle, slower and stupider). Darwin argued that beneficial random variations formed the raw creative material for evolution.

But something else was required to take this raw material and build it into new forms of life. Darwin believed he had found it in nature "red in tooth and claw."[1] When living things reproduce, they not only introduce random variations into their offspring, they usually produce more offspring than can survive and go on to reproduce. Food shortages, predators, disease and other threats cull the offspring of every species. Darwin called this *natural selection*. The environment "selects" some organisms to survive and reproduce, and it "selects" others to be somebody's lunch. Or to put it in less colloquial terms, random variation produces organisms with different strengths and weaknesses. Natural selection then selects those organisms best suited to their environment, organisms that survive, reproduce and pass on their helpful evolutionary variations.

Neither the random variations nor the natural selection are the controversial part of Darwin's theory. Then as now, it was obvious that creatures vary from their parents and that nature often weeds out poorly adapted creatures while allowing the stronger or faster or smarter offspring to survive. The controversial part was Darwin's proposal that natural selection working on random variations evolved all of the living forms around us. He insisted that random variations and natural selection, working in tandem, could take the first living cell and, from this, evolve our planet's menagerie of plants and animals, all without the need for intelligent guidance. Today, Darwinism dominates historical biology. Some will claim that modern Darwinism is just one of several competing modern evolutionary theories, but the fact is, amid their real differences, all mainstream evolutionary theories appeal to the twin mechanisms of random variation and natural selection to do the primary work of building new kinds of plants and animals.

FROM DARWIN TO THE DEATH OF GOD
Darwin was a skillful writer and defender of his theory, and it quickly grew in popularity. Some believers in God integrated

Darwin's theory into their faith. Others saw it as powerful new evidence that there was no Creator. Oxford biologist Richard Dawkins summed it up well: "Darwin made it possible to be an intellectually fulfilled atheist."[2]

Darwin's influence didn't stop there. By providing what many regarded as the last missing piece in the billiard-ball picture of reality (materialism), his theory of evolution gradually transformed every facet of our culture—law, politics, art, literature, education, even music. As atheist philosopher Daniel Dennett put it, Darwinism is a "universal acid" that "eats through just about every traditional concept, and leaves in its wake a revolutionized world-view, with most of the old landmarks still recognizable, but transformed in fundamental ways."[3]

DARWIN AS DOGMA

After a century and a half, this "revolutionized world-view" isn't very revolutionary. Now it's the dominant view among academics, and the proponents of intelligent design have dared to suggest an alternative explanation. If we had been willing to present our case for intelligent design as a religious argument rooted in this or that holy book, the Darwinists would happily have ignored us. But we have worked to show that the case for intelligent design is based on physical evidence and tools of reasoning available to anyone, regardless of creed.

How have Darwinists responded? A few have responded with civility and a refreshing willingness to engage in civil debate. Unfortunately, many prominent Darwinists have taken a different tack. The leading defenders of modern Darwinism have tried by every means available to avoid an open contest of ideas with intelligent design. They've distorted our arguments to the press;

pushed journalists to stop covering the intelligent design controversy; tried to get ID scientists fired; and even sued a school district that dared to mention to students that an alternative theory—intelligent design—existed.

DARWINISM BY DEFINITION

The Darwinists' favorite tactic for avoiding an open contest of ideas is to label intelligent design *nonscience*. For instance, a thinly veiled editorial on the front page of the *Washington Post* labeled ID "Not Science, Politics."[4] In that story, Barry Lynn, the director of Americans United for Separation of Church and State, insisted that intelligent design is merely "a veneer over a certain theological message," thus identifying intelligent design not with science but with religion.

The question is, do these claims hold water? The controversy surrounding intelligent design occurs at many levels, but ultimately it's a scientific controversy within the scientific community. There are several indicators of this. One indicator is that the researchers developing the theory of intelligent design (design theorists) have a growing program of scientific research and are now publishing research supporting intelligent design in the peer-reviewed mainstream scientific literature, especially in the biological literature.[5] A related indicator is that increasingly their work is being studied and critiqued within the mainstream scientific literature.[6]

Despite this, critics of intelligent design continue to insist that intelligent design is not a scientific theory since it violates methodological materialism. Darwin himself invoked this rule to defend his theory against the design position, and Darwinists have been using it ever since. Eugenie Scott, director of a pro-evolution watchdog group and a leading critic of intelligent design, makes the case for methodological materialism this way:

> Most scientists today require that science be carried out according to the rule of *methodological materialism*: to explain the natural world scientifically, scientists must restrict themselves only to material causes (to matter, energy, and their interaction). There is a practical reason for this restriction: it works. By continuing to seek natural explanations for how the world works, we have been able to find them. If supernatural explanations are allowed, they will discourage—or at least delay—the discovery of natural explanations, and we will understand less about the universe.[7]

But what if the "natural explanation" for something isn't the true explanation? What if the true cause for, say, the origin of the universe was a creative intelligence at work? Scott's case for methodological materialism just assumes that the correct explanations for everything in nature will turn out to be purely material explanations, blind forces. But that's the thing at issue. Scott is committing a logical fallacy that students are taught to avoid in freshman English—*begging the question*.

Certainly the universe operates according to an astonishing variety of material causes—the interaction of what physicists refer to as *laws* and *constants*. But the defender of methodological materialism must do more than show that many or even most features of the universe are directed by such material regularities. They must show that clearly all features of the universe were caused by such material forces. Why this burden of proof? Because if it's even reasonably possible that a creative intelligence played a role in the origin of certain things in nature, then refusing to consider the possibility amounts to willed blindness.

WILL THE REAL SHRINKING GAP PLEASE STAND UP?

Faced with such an objection, the defenders of methodological materialism tend to revert to their story of scientific progress. It runs like this: *Humans used to attribute every mysterious force in nature to the activity of one or more gods. They stuffed a god into any knowledge gap they had about the natural world, shrugged and moved on. Those mysterious gaps have been shrinking with every passing generation. Granted, no one could prove that every feature of the universe derived from purely material causes, but any reasonable person who has followed the progress of science can see where things are headed—toward an ever-shrinking and eventually vanishing god of the gaps.*

The problem with this oft-repeated story is that it misrepresents modern scientific history. In other words, it's bogus. First, it incorrectly implies that belief in an active God has been nothing but a drag on scientific progress. In fact—and there is a broad agreement among historians of science on this—belief that the world is the rational product of a rational maker inspired men like Copernicus, Galileo, Kepler and Newton to search for and begin finding the underlying laws of nature. As Copernicus put it, he was seeking to uncover "the mechanism of the universe, wrought for us by a supremely good and orderly creator."[8]

Second, the evidence for intelligent design has not been shrinking over the last two centuries. It's been growing. This is especially obvious in two areas: how scientists explain the origin of life, and how they explain the existence of the universe.

STORIES THAT WEREN'T

In Darwin's time the conventional wisdom among scientists was that microscopic life was simple, little more than tiny sacks of

Jell-O. There was also a widespread belief in spontaneous generation, the idea that creatures could spontaneously arise out of everything—from rotting meat to the dew that falls on plants. A series of discoveries in the seventeenth and eighteenth centuries began to chip away at this conventional wisdom, and in 1861 Louis Pasteur conducted a series of experiments that put the idea of spontaneous generation to rest once and for all. Then in the next century scientists began amassing evidence of just how complex even the simplest life is, with even one-celled organisms emerging as microminiaturized factories of unparalleled sophistication. What had seemed like something that the blind forces of nature might easily throw together—the first one-celled organism—now looked, for all the world, like the handiwork of a master engineer.

In Darwin's time scientists "in the know" also assumed that the universe was eternal. If that was the case, there was no mystery about the origin of matter since matter had always existed. However, developments in physics and astronomy eventually overturned that notion. Based on a substantial and compelling body of scientific evidence, scientists now are in broad agreement that our universe came into being. What scientists thought needed no explanation—the origin of matter—suddenly cried out for an explanation.

Yes, scientists continue to gain new insights into how material forces cause various things in nature. But the process of discovery is a two-way street. In Darwin's time, scientists thought the origin of life and the existence of matter were easily explained within the confines of methodological materialism. Now, 150 years later, methodological materialists are at a loss: they can give no adequate, purely material cause for the origin of life or for the origin of matter.

The defenders of methodological materialism will insist that considering intelligent design for the origin of life is "giving up." But give up on what? Design theorists are seeking to follow the physical evidence to true explanations about the origin of various things in nature. The only thing we're giving up on is an artificial and dogmatic rule that hinders the free pursuit of that goal.

To further illustrate the difference between the two approaches to scientific investigation, consider again the laws and constants of nature, things like gravity, electromagnetism and the forces that hold atoms together. In the latter half of the twentieth century, evidence began piling up that these laws and constants appear finely calibrated to allow for life. Researchers discovered that if any one of these constants were even a little different, life would be impossible in our universe. Not just life on Earth but any kind of complex life: Martian, Vulcan, Wookie—pick a space film and fill in the blank. The narrow range of settings that make for a habitable universe are so rare among the total set of possible arrangements that physicists have taken to calling it *the fine-tuning problem*.

Many leading astronomers and physicists have responded by suggesting that the universe is fine tuned because, well, it was fine tuned. That is, a creative intelligence was involved in deliberately setting the constants of nature to allow for life. Nobel laureate Arno Penzias put it this way:

> Astronomy leads us to a unique event, a universe which was created out of nothing, one with the very delicate balance needed to provide exactly the conditions required to permit life, and one which has an underlying (one might say "supernatural") plan. Thus, the observations of modern science seem to lead to the same conclusions as centuries-old intuition.[9]

Members of the intelligent design community, design theorists such as Guillermo Gonzalez, Jay Richards and William Lane Craig, have further developed the argument as a rigorous inference to the best explanation.[10]

The strict methodological materialist will refuse to consider the possibility of intelligent design in this case. Our central point here is that this unwillingness is itself unreasonable. But note that it's also inconsistent, since on the one hand they say scientists shouldn't consider the possibility, but on the other hand they offer arguments against design as an explanation for fine tuning. If we're not even supposed to consider the possibility, why assess the arguments for it? Finally, the arguments they give against the design explanation in this case are clearly defective. Let's look at each of them in turn.

THE FIRING-SQUAD FALLACY

One strategy for countering the fine-tuning evidence for design runs like this: *Of course the universe is fine-tuned for complex life. Otherwise we wouldn't be here to notice our good fortune.* Call this the firing-squad fallacy. The prisoner shuts his eyes. The rifle shots are fired. Unharmed, the prisoner opens his eyes and discovers a perfect bullet pattern outlining his body on the wall behind him. The friendly guard congratulates him. "Hey, it looks like the firing squad had orders to miss!" The prisoner shakes his head. "No, it was just dumb luck. If they hadn't missed, I wouldn't be here to comment on my good fortune."[11]

This is the same faulty argument regularly trotted out to explain away the fine-tuning pattern in physics. Question: What type of cause has the demonstrated power to produce the fine-tuning pattern? Answer: We wouldn't be here to observe the pattern if the pattern didn't exist. That's the firing-squad fallacy: pointing to *a necessary condition* for observing X when what's being sought is a *sufficient cause* for X. Instead of offering a sufficient cause for the origin of the fine-tuning pattern, opponents of intelligent design change the subject.

THE GAMBLER'S FALLACY

A second strategy for explaining away the fine-tuning evidence for design runs like this: *Our universe is just one of countless billions of universes that have popped into existence; ours is just one of the few with the right parameters for life.* If you're wondering what they are basing this claim of billions of other universes on, that's a good question. This response shows just how keen some are to explain away the evidence of design in the universe. The only universe we have a good reason to think exists is the one around us. The only reason to assume bazillions of other universes *must* exist is if one insists as a point of dogma that the fine-tuning evidence for design *must* be illusory.

The multiple-universe explanation commits what's called the gambler's fallacy. A gambler is at a casino table beside a mob boss. The mobster loses a couple of hands and then glares at the dealer. On the next two hands the mobster lays down royal flushes, each time without exchanging any cards. The other players wisely compliment the mob boss on his good fortune, cash in their chips and leave. But the gambler beside the Mafioso stays in the game, a look of wonder spreading across his face. On the next hand the mob boss lays down a third royal flush. The gambler beside him whips out a calculator, punches in a few numbers, and then exclaims, "Wow, the odds of that happening three times in a row are 1 in 274,294,315,000,000,000. Just think how many people around the world—heck, around the galaxy!—must be playing poker right now to make that run of luck possible!"

The naive gambler hasn't explained the mob boss's "run of luck." He's simply overlooked the best explanation: intelligent design. This is the same error committed by those who appeal to multiple, undetectable universes to explain away the "run of luck" that gave us a universe fine-tuned for life.

MINORITY REPORT

Besides appealing to methodological materialism, critics of intelligent design employ several other arguments to paint ID as nonscience. One of their favorites is to insist that ID doesn't qualify as science because it's a minority position. This may be their silliest argument. Science is not decided by majority vote. The majority of scientists can and have been wrong about scientific matters. In his *Structure of Scientific Revolutions*, historian and philosopher of science Thomas Kuhn documented numerous reversals in science where views once confidently held by the scientific community ended up being discarded and replaced.[12] For instance, until the theory of plate tectonics was proposed, geologists used to believe the continents were immovable.[13] In the nineteenth and early twentieth centuries, most astronomers also assumed that the universe was eternal. In fact, many persisted in believing this in the face of strong evidence to the contrary, including evidence from thermodynamics and later from discoveries by Albert Einstein, Edwin Hubble and others. If we want to talk about suspect arguments, then let's talk about arguing for a theory based on appeals to some real or imagined consensus. Author Michael Crichton had this to say on the subject in a speech about global warming:

> Historically, the claim of consensus has been the first refuge of scoundrels; it is a way to avoid debate by claiming that the matter is already settled. Whenever you hear the

consensus of scientists agrees on something or other, reach for your wallet, because you're being had. Let's be clear: the work of science has nothing whatever to do with consensus. Consensus is the business of politics. Science, on the contrary, requires only one investigator who happens to be right, which means that he or she has results that are verifiable by reference to the real world. In science consensus is irrelevant. What is relevant is reproducible results. The greatest scientists in history are great precisely because they broke with the consensus. There is no such thing as consensus science. If it's consensus, it isn't science. If it's science, it isn't consensus. Period.[14]

DOCTORS FOR DESIGN

There is a fundamental problem with invoking consensus to win a science debate. This is all the more clear when highly educated and accomplished scientists represent a minority view. Indeed, various highly educated biologists with impressive records of accomplishment take an intelligent design position. (We'll hear from some of them in the course of this book.) And many of the most respected physicists in the world have suggested that they see design as the best explanation for the fine-tuning of the laws and constants of nature. Finally, a poll by the Finkelstein Institute found that some 60 percent of U.S. medical doctors think that intelligent design played some role in the origin of humans. Many Darwinists tell us that nothing in biology makes sense except in the light of Darwinian evolution. Apparently, these doctors didn't get the memo. Of course, Darwinists could write off these doctors as something other than "real scientists," but this tactic rings hollow given medical doctors' obvious expertise in human biology.

Darwinists might also insist that the 60 percent majority was simply a cabal of Christian fundamentalist doctors, but the poll's demographic breakdown suggests otherwise. If you're able, go to the Finkelstein poll link at <http://web.archive.org/web/20061017043539/www.hcdi.net/polls/J5776/> and click on Q7 in the left-hand margin: "What are your views on the origin and development of human beings?" Only the third answer fits within the Darwinian view of evolution by natural selection. That is, the third answer covers every evolutionary model in biology that appeals to strictly natural causes. The other two answers both see a role for a creative intelligence in the origin of humans. Here's how the poll results breaks down demographically:

- Jewish doctors: 32 percent reject Darwinism
- Protestant doctors (largest group of U.S. doctors): 81 percent reject Darwinism
- Catholic doctors: 78 percent reject Darwinism
- Orthodox Christian doctors: 72 percent reject Darwinism
- Hindu doctors: 54 percent reject Darwinism
- Buddhist doctors: 43 percent reject Darwinism (compared to 36 percent who accept it)
- Muslim doctors: 86 percent reject Darwinism
- Atheist doctors: 2 percent reject Darwinism
- "Spiritual but no organized religion": 48 percent reject Darwinism
- "Other": 54 percent reject Darwinism[15]

Although the margin of error is surely much higher for the small sampling of Hindus, Buddhists, Spiritual and Other, the results for even these groups should give anyone pause who has been told that only Christian fundamentalists reject Darwinism and see evidence of design in biology.

THE SIN OF SIGNIFICANCE

Another argument Darwinists sometimes use is to assert that ID isn't science because it has religious, philosophical and political implications. The problem is that this standard also disqualifies Darwinism. As we've already seen, Darwinism is literally ooz-ing with larger cultural implications, so much so that Dennett, himself a Darwinist, calls it a "universal acid." And Dennett is by no means a lone voice on the subject. According to the late Harvard evolutionist Stephen Jay Gould, "Biology took away our status as paragons created in the image of God. . . . Before Darwin, we thought that a benevolent God had created us."[16] In *A Darwinian Left: Politics, Evolution, and Cooperation*, Prince-ton bioethicist Peter Singer remarks that we must "face the fact that we are evolved animals and that we bear the evidence of our inheritance, not only in our anatomy and our DNA, but in our behavior too."[17]

These men are drawing religious, philosophical and political implications from evolutionary theory. We could fill a book with this sort of thing, and the instances stretch all the way back to Darwin's time. Darwin's leading defender in the Victorian age, Thomas Huxley, launched the X Club, a group focused on prop-agating Darwin's theory of evolution, in part because they were attracted to the theological, philosophical and political implica-tions of Darwin's theory.

Does any of this make evolutionary theory unscientific? No. By the same token, intelligent design's implications do not ren-der it unscientific.[18]

DESIGN DETECTIVES

When we read the typical newspaper article about intelligent design, we get the impression that the design theorist is an unimaginative fellow thinking, *Gee, I can't see how an eye or a bat or a butterfly could have randomly evolved. They're just too darned complicated. Heck, that right there proves evolution is kooky and somebody designed 'em.* Critics of ID are good at showing just how stupid such an argument is. But if we look closer, we'll notice the straw sticking out of the spot just below the argument's neck where the clip-on tie has come loose. This is what logicians call a straw man. It's not the real ID argument. Instead, the critics go after a straw man of the real argument, presumably because it's easier to knock down. The danger, of course, is that the audience may look too closely and discover the charade and realize that the actual theory of intelligent design is something else entirely.

To remain open to the possibility of design is the call of the intelligent design movement. It's a call to apply consistently the methods used in two types of science: science concerned with information, and science that looks for the past causes of present clues.

Many special sciences already employ the concept of design and would be inconceivable without it. These include artificial intelligence, the science of code making and code breaking (cryptography), and the science of random number generation (used for video games and many other things).

Or take criminal investigation. Detectives employ sophisticated technology, careful observation and logical analysis to discover the best explanation for something that happened in the past. They find a body and ask, Did this person die from an illness, from an accident or from foul play? That is, was the person killed by some unintended event or by design? Was the person murdered? Unless they have been paid off by someone, detectives in such cases don't rule out death by design before they've studied the scene. They keep an open mind and follow the clues in search of the best explanation.

Design theorists do the same thing. We look at the finely tuned constants of nature, the sophisticated machinery inside living cells or the genetic information needed to build those machines, and we ask, Did these things arise by accident or by design? Then we follow the evidence.

DAMS, ALIENS AND CHEATS

Intelligent design doesn't always refer to human design either. Some animals display intelligence and can design things that the discerning eye recognizes as designed, such as the cleverly constructed dams that beavers build. The science of design detection isn't even confined to Earth. The search for extraterrestrial intelligence (SETI) looks for signs of intelligence in radio signals from outer space. SETI researchers assume that among all the naturally occurring radio waves in outer space, we may be able to distinguish those that are designed from those that occur naturally. And Francis Crick, one of the scientists who discovered DNA's structure, has even proposed that life is too intricate to have arisen here on planet Earth and so must have been deliberately seeded by some extraterrestrial civilization.[19] Though regarded as wildly implausible by many, his theory still falls within the bounds of science.

Science itself needs to employ the concept of design to keep itself honest. For instance, falsifying data and presenting other people's work as our own (plagiarism) are far more common in science than some would like to admit.[20] What keeps these abuses in check is our ability to detect these unethical designs. If design is so readily detectable within various special sciences, and our ability to detect it is one of the key things keeping scientists honest, why should the normal methods of design detection be barred from the science of biology?

A HISTORICAL SCIENCE

The theory of intelligent design looks at patterns in nature with the clear signature of design. As philosopher of science Stephen Meyer notes, the theory of intelligent design is like other arguments in the historical sciences in that it's a comparative argument, an argument to the best explanation. There are many competing explanations for things like the origin of life, but they all fall into two broad categories—intelligent cause explanations and material cause explanations. According to the theory of intelligent design, an intelligent cause (a mind at work) is the best explanation for certain features of the natural world. Why? Intelligence is the only type of cause with the demonstrated power to produce things like new information (such as we find in DNA) or complex machines that require all of their parts to function (like the rotary engines bacteria use to get around).

Intelligent design isn't a gee-whiz hunch but a testable scientific theory based on precise methods and our everyday experience of successfully detecting design in things around us. ID does argue that there are major problems with Darwinism, but it goes much further:

- ID critiques not only Darwinism but every leading evolutionary theory that leaves a designer out of the story of life's origin and development.

- ID reaches beyond biology to chemistry, physics and astronomy.

- ID offers abundant *positive evidence* that some patterns in nature are the product of a creative intelligence.

Design theorists look at things as vast as the laws of nature and as tiny as the rotary engines that bacteria use to motor through liquid. Then they ask a couple of questions. Is it logically possible these things were designed? If so, is there any way we could tell by studying them and the world around us?

Many ID opponents answer *no* to both questions. They say that real scientists, whatever their religious beliefs, must bracket off the possibility of intelligent design while doing science. And they insist that even if some things in nature were designed, there would be no way to tell apart from divine revelation. Design theorists answer the first and second question with *yes* and *yes*. (1) It's at least logically possible that some things in nature were designed. And (2) it's logically possible that such things bear evidence of having been designed. To grasp how modest and reasonable these two claims are, imagine someone asserting the opposite: *It isn't even logically possible that some things in nature were designed, and even if some things were, it isn't logically possible that such things bear evidence of having been designed.* Even many nonreligious people, including agnostics, would find such a position plainly wrongheaded.

If we reject this *no* and *no* position, where should we go from here? We suggest that if it's at least logically possible to detect real design in nature, we ought to go to nature and see if there is clear evidence for design rather than ruling the possibility out of court beforehand.

Since the vast majority of people—including highly educated people—agree, surely there is room for a broad public conversation about the possible evidence for intelligent design. The conversation has two sides. On the one side, some hold that a careful look at nature reveals no evidence of intelligent design. On the other side, some hold that a careful look at certain things in nature does reveal the signature of intelligent design.

APPEARANCE VERSUS REALITY

Drive across the Black Hills of South Dakota and you'll come across a rock formation that bears the unmistakable mark of intelligent design. The formation is Mount Rushmore, the towering likenesses of four U.S. presidents carved in stone. Now drive to Arizona and turn north from I-40 west of Flagstaff and you'll come across another rock formation, the Grand Canyon. As remarkable as the canyon is, there's no reason to think a sculptor or engineer built it.

Not all rock formations are so obviously designed and not designed as Mount Rushmore and the Grand Canyon. Take, for instance, the Old Man of the Mountain, a stone formation in the White Mountains of New Hampshire that resembles a human face. Nineteenth-century American novelist Nathaniel Hawthorne described it as a "Great Stone face" that looked as if "an enormous giant, or a Titan, had sculpted his own likeness on the precipice."[21] When viewed from just the right angle from just the right distance, it looks designed. But it isn't. Natural forces acting blindly and without intelligence or foresight just happened to produce it, much as natural forces sometimes sculpt a cloud to look like a rabbit, a whale or some other animal.

Here we have three kinds of rock formations. Mount Rushmore looks designed, and is. The Grand Canyon doesn't look

Figure 2.1. Mount Rushmore

Figure 2.2. The Grand Canyon

designed, and isn't. And the Old Man of the Mountain looks designed, but isn't. Of course, there's one other possibility: a rock formation that doesn't look designed but is. Finding such objects is the job of archaeologists. Crude arrowheads and weathered burial mounds can look like natural objects to the untrained eye, but a good

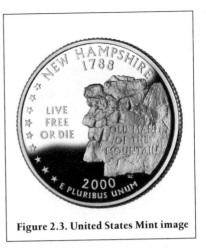

Figure 2.3. United States Mint image

archaeologist spots the evidence of design that others miss.

Figure 2.4. A crude arrowhead?

These four rock formations represent four main groups: designed and appears designed, not designed but appears designed, designed but appears undesigned, not designed and appears undesigned (see table 2.1).

We use rock formations to illustrate these four categories, but the categories cover everything anyone has ever seen. On the one hand, things can *appear* to be either designed or not designed. On the other hand, a particular thing either was designed by someone (or some team), or it wasn't.

Look again at table 2.1, but this time with the four possibilities numbered (see table 2.2).

Figure 2.5. Weathered burial mounds

Table 2.1. Four Categories of Rock Formations

	Really Designed	Really Undesigned
Appears Designed	Mount Rushmore	Old Man of the Mountain
Appears Undesigned	Burial Mound	Grand Canyon

Table 2.2. Four Categories of Material Objects

	Really Designed	Really Undesigned
Appears Designed	1.	2.
Appears Undesigned	3.	4.

Boxes 1 and 4 pose no problem. If something looks designed and is designed (box 1) or looks undesigned and is undesigned (box 4), appearance and reality match.

Boxes 2 and 3 are trickier. With them, appearances are deceiving, at least to the untrained eye. The challenge in such cases is to tell appearance from reality. And because we know such cases don't have a big "Box 2" or "Box 3" sign hanging around their necks, a careful investigator will be on guard against deceiving appearances.

The sun looks like it rises in the east and sets in the west, but really the Earth spins on its axis as it revolves around the sun. A healthy skepticism about appearances is vital.

At the same time, it can't be an indiscriminate skepticism. Sometimes appearances and reality match. During a solar eclipse, the moon appears to be nearer than the sun and, as it turns out, it is. In this case, appearance and reality agree. To distinguish appearance from reality, the successful investigator must remain open to various possibilities and follow the evidence.

What about the case of plants and animals? Biologists readily agree that living things appear designed. The lens of a human eye is like the lens of a camera. The human heart is as much a pump as any humanly constructed pump, only more intricate. And the microscopic bacterial flagellum is an amazing rotary engine that puts the well-designed rotary engines of the Mazda Corporation to shame. Oxford zoologist and atheist Richard Dawkins summarizes the matter this way: "Biology is the study of complicated things that give the appearance of having been designed for a purpose."[22]

How should we respond to this strong appearance of design? Does the biological realm lie behind box 1 or box 2? Is the appearance of design in biology real or merely apparent? One way to answer the question is to insist that scientists aren't allowed to consider the possibility that the appearance of design in biology is real. Francis Crick, one of the scientists who discovered the winding staircase structure of DNA, the molecule that stores genetic information, once urged biologists to "constantly keep in mind that what they see was not designed, but rather evolved."[23] Design theorists recommend a different approach: Remain open to the possibility that livings things appear designed because they are designed, and then probe for clues that could answer the question.

3

The World's Smallest
Rotary Engine

IN CHAPTER ONE THE CAPTAIN and pilot in our voyage into the cell argued over the tiny outboard motor called the bacterial flagellum. The characters were fictional, but they were rehashing a real scientific debate, one that has spilled onto the pages of the world's most prestigious science journals and into newspapers like the *New York Times*, *Washington Post* and *USA Today*. Let's consider exactly what the two sides are saying, boiling it down into everyday language.

The most prominent design theorist in the debate is Lehigh University biochemist Michael Behe, author of the bestselling *Darwin's Black Box*. His most visible opponent is Brown University biologist Kenneth Miller. Miller is coauthor of a high school biology textbook and perhaps intelligent design's most capable opponent. Some ID critics try to dismiss intelligent design simply by labeling it "religion" or "bad philosophy." Miller attempts this as well, but he deserves credit for also trying to address Behe's actual arguments.[1]

Miller makes three main objections. He says Behe's case is based on what the scientific community doesn't know, whereas it should be based on what we do know. His second and closely related objection is that Behe improperly invokes God to explain scientific mysteries. Instead, Miller says, scientists should keep looking for a natural explanation. And finally Miller insists that the bacterial flagellum motor actually can be built up one small step at a time through random variations and natural selection.

Miller's arguments look good from a distance, but they fall apart on close inspection.

MILLER OBJECTION 1: A GEE-WHIZ ARGUMENT

Miller claims that the problem with design theorists like Behe is a failure of the imagination. As he says, design theorists can't "imagine how evolutionary mechanisms might have produced a certain species, organ, or structure," so they dismiss the possibility. But Miller is mistaken. It isn't that design theorists can't imagine how those machines arose. Part of Behe's argument (and only part of it) is that no one has imagined how they might have arisen naturally, much less demonstrated an evolutionary scenario for them in the lab.

To really imagine something means to see it in rich detail. In this full sense of *imagine*, the Darwinists haven't imagined an evolutionary pathway for the bacterial flagellum motor, much less tested it in the lab and shown it to be sound. Theirs is a tale as vague as it is implausible.

MILLER OBJECTION 2: THE GOD OF THE GAPS

Miller reminds us that science would never have gone anywhere if it had attributed every natural mystery to divine action. For instance, science might never have discovered the natural cause of lightning if it had gone on assuming these were bolts flung down by the gods. As primitive and superstitious as that attitude sounds, Miller says this is just the sort of god-of-the-gaps reasoning that modern design theorists use. He claims that we reason straight from the premise "Shucks, no one has figured out how the flagellum arose" to the conclusion, "Gee, a cosmic designer must've done it."

Miller is debating a straw man. What follows is the actual argument.

Certain biological systems have a feature called *irreducible complexity*. That's a fancy phrase for a simple idea. Think of a mousetrap. It needs all of its parts before it can so much as bruise a mouse. Intelligent agents (engineers) build irreducibly complex things all the time. In fact, any time we discover this sort of machine and can trace it back to its source, we always arrive at a mind or minds (Thomas Edison, Alexander Graham Bell, the Wright brothers). But we also find irreducible complexity in living things, and that's a problem for Darwinists. Darwinists don't have a clue how biological systems with this feature first arose (Miller disputes this, but we'll come back to that). In fact, humankind has no direct experience of any purely mindless cause ever producing a new kind of irreducibly complex system or device.

At this point, Darwinists insist that everyone must maintain faith in modern evolutionary theory, must go on looking for a way to make the evidence fit their model of mindless evolution. But there is another way to respond to the evidence, one that has deep roots in the history of scientific progress.

A geologist might try to explain where a layer of lava ash in someone's garden soil came from. An archaeologist might try to explain how that ancient and imposing structure on the Salisbury Plain of England, known as Stonehenge, came to be. An astronomer might try to figure out why the universe is expanding. Each of these researchers is doing what's called *historical science*. They are trying to identify causes in the distant past that we can't observe. If they can't observe the cause directly, what can they do? Charles Lyell, one of the founders of modern geology, said that historical scientists should seek to explain past events "by reference to causes now in operation."[2] He meant that they should search for a *type* of cause, active in the present, with the demonstrated power to have caused the past event.

For example, what carved out the Royal Gorge in Colorado? Was it an earthquake that split the rock? Or did the Arkansas River carve it? Assembling all of the available evidence, geologists have concluded that only the second option, a river, has the demonstrated power to have caused the set of features that make up the Royal Gorge.

Keep in mind that when Lyell talked about "causes now in operation," he meant *types of causes* now in operation. Even if the Arkansas River had been dry since before the first Indians came to Colorado, geologists could still determine that one *type* of cause, erosion caused by flowing water, was the best explanation for the Royal Gorge. They wouldn't need to produce a particular flowing river right in front of our eyes in order to make their case that a river of some sort did it. They would just need to point to the telltale signs of river erosion and demonstrate that their explanation was better than the competing explanations.

Return now to machines like mousetraps that need all of their parts to work. What around us has the demonstrated power to produce these kinds of machines? We know of only one type of cause that produces such machines: intelligent design. Examples are all around us—mousetraps, motorcycle engines, the integrated circuits in computers. So what is the best explanation for the origin of biological systems with this same characteristic of irreducible complexity? Intelligent design. This is the positive evidence for intelligent design.

Despite Miller's claim to the contrary, intelligent design isn't an argument from ignorance but an argument based on our common knowledge. When we attribute intelligent design to complex biological machines that need all of their parts to work, we're doing what historical scientists do generally. Think of it as a three-step process: (1) locate a type of cause active in the present that routinely produces the thing in question; (2) make a thorough search to determine if it is the only known cause of this type of thing; and (3) if it is, offer it as the best explanation for the thing in question. Here the task is helped along by the fact that there is only one type of cause known to produce irreducibly complex machines—intelligent design.

MILLER OBJECTION 3: THE BACTERIAL FLAGELLUM MOTOR ISN'T IRREDUCIBLY COMPLEX

But Miller has a more direct objection to Behe's argument. Miller insists that the bacterial flagellum motor isn't irreducibly complex, and the Darwinian mechanism could have built it one small step at a time.[3] To illustrate, he takes Behe's mousetrap illustration and turns it on its head, noting that three of the mousetrap's components could make for a dandy tie clip and two could work as a clipboard. This is how evolution arrived at a sophisticated rotary engine, Miller argues, by taking a series of biological machines from other systems on the way to the bacterial flagellum. Nature is a scavenger, he says, cobbling together parts from existing machines for new purposes.[4]

But Miller has only illustrated the obvious: just about any complex machine we find contains parts that a good mechanic could use for some other purpose. It's why born mechanics hate to discard broken-down machinery. They never know when they might be able to scavenge a part from it for some new project. But notice who's doing the scavenging and the building. Not the parts. Not the grease. Not the garage or the wind whistling through the garage. No, it's the mechanic in the garage. What is the one thing in our experience that co-opts irreducibly complex machines and uses their parts to build a new and more intricate machine? Intelligent agents.

So Miller's illustration actually works against his own position. Mike Gene points out another flaw in Miller's logic:

> What is interesting about this logic is that we already know that the mousetrap was intelligently designed. We also know that it did not first exist as a clipboard, then a tie clip. Thus, while it is logically possible to see the mousetrap as Miller does, that is, as a modified clipboard and tie clip, such perceptions are not tied to history nor the origin of the mousetrap. Thus, coming up with imaginary accounts . . . is rather meaningless. If we can successfully come up with such explanations where they are known to be false (the mousetrap), how do we know that our ability to do likewise with things like the flagellum are not also inherently flawed?[5]

Worse, Miller's proposed evolutionary path to the flagellum is even sketchier than his mousetrap evolution scenario. Miller bases it on a microscopic syringe that pokes holes in passing cells, and then it squirts some nasty stuff in that hijacks their machinery.[6] The technical name for this biological machine is the type III secretory system (or TTSS). Here we'll just refer to it as a microsyringe. About ten different proteins are needed to code this mean little machine, and each of these proteins is similar to proteins in the bacterial flagellum motor. Miller argues that nature could have selected this microsyringe as an ancestor on the evolutionary path to the flagellum, but his argument has big problems.

Imagine if all the protein parts just happened to be hanging around waiting to be assembled into a bacterial flagellum motor—not just the ten protein parts from the microsyringe but all forty necessary parts. Even if that unlikely event occurred, the parts would still have to come together just so. Each would have to be added to the emerging motor at just the right time and in just the right position in the way an automobile engine gets assembled. The car engine illustration is doubly helpful here because it gets us past thinking of the forty protein parts as akin to simple wooden blocks. In fact, they are far more intricate than many of the parts we find in a car engine. We may have all the parts on hand, but we still need some hands—one or more intelligent designers—to assemble them.

And this is only half the problem for Miller and his fellow design critics. Look at how a bacterial flagellum is assembled today. Sophisticated microscopes have revealed that the flagellum's cellular factory has an elaborate system of DNA instructions (the software) along with many protein machines to choreograph and build the sophisticated bacterial flagellum motor in just the right order for success. As researchers have noted, this tiny factory may itself be irreducibly complex.[7]

The Darwinists need a credible evolutionary path to the bacterial flagellum *and* to the sophisticated factory that builds them. They don't have either.

At best, the microsyringe Miller points to represents one possible step in a Darwinian evolutionary path to the bacterial flagellum. But what's needed is a complete evolutionary path, not just one possible step along the way. To claim otherwise is like saying we can travel by foot from Los Angeles to the Philippine Islands because we've discovered the Hawaiian Islands in between. Evolutionary biology needs to do better than that.

There's another problem with Miller's scenario, and it's a big one. The best current evidence in biology suggests that the microsyringe appeared after the bacterial flagellum motor and not the other way around.[8] That means the microsyringe doesn't provide even an isolated step in the supposed evolution of the motor.

There's more. The motor doesn't even help explain the Darwinian evolution of the simpler syringe. After all, the syringe is much simpler than the bacterial flagellum motor. It contains about ten proteins similar to proteins in the motor. The motor requires an additional thirty or more proteins, which are unique. Darwinian evolution is trying to explain how complex life forms arose from simpler ones, beginning with a single-celled organism. But if the syringe developed from the motor, then all the Darwinists have done is explain the simpler in terms of the more complex.

FLAGELLAR FOLLIES

Evolutionist Theodosius Dobzhansky once said, "Nothing in biology makes sense except in the light of evolution."[9] In fact, Darwin's theory offers no insight into how the bacterial flagellum motor arose. If Darwinists had even an inkling how such systems arose by blind processes, Miller would not—more than a decade after the publication of Behe's *Darwin's Black Box*—still be lamely gesturing at a microsyringe, holding it up as a possible evolutionary ancestor to the bacterial flagellum. Instead, he would simply provide a detailed explanation of how a system like the bacterial flagellum motor arose by Darwinian means.

And it isn't as if the Darwinists haven't tried to find an evolutionary pathway for the bacterial flagellum. They've made a long, concerted effort to imagine a detailed, credible evolutionary pathway to this motor.[10] Despite such efforts, their most detailed evolutionary stories remain hopelessly vague, and the few parts of the story that aren't vague are riddled with serious problems.[11]

DARWINIST LOGIC MEETS THE MONA LISA

We've just waded through a bit of heavy scientific back-and-forth. So now for something completely different. Consider the grassy likeness of the Mona Lisa in figure 3.1.

Figure 3.1. Mona Lisa grass

Is it the product of design or blind evolution? Science writer Casey Luskin, tongue-planted-firmly-in-cheek, offers the following analysis:

> Before you infer intelligent design, keep in mind that grass-cutting shears share an extremely high similarity with

scissors which are used to cut paper. Since a paper stencil was apparently used in the origination of the grass-pattern, it's likely that a pair of scissors was used to cut the stencil. This makes it plausible to assume that the grass-cutting shears were co-opted from scissors, because both are clearly homologous structures based upon their similarity. Moreover, paper is made of plant material, and grass is a plant. This could account for the origin of the stencil itself. Finally, Virginia has metal resources which could account for the origin of the original scissors. Don't use a science-stopping explanation and infer design! We're "on our way" to figuring this out, so don't threaten the progress of science, medicine, and all of civilization by saying this was designed! You might as well reject round earth "theory" and the Periodic Table![12]

THE CLUE THAT ISN'T

If you enjoyed the grassy Mona Lisa illustration, consider another one on the whimsical end of the spectrum. A couple of kids are stargazing on the sidewalk in front of their houses. After a few minutes, the boy announces to the girl that one day he will climb to Jupiter because he's sure there's a natural ladder stretching from Earth to Jupiter. The girl points out that nobody on Earth has ever found such a ladder. She further notes that there are other good reasons to conclude it doesn't exist—the constantly changing distance between the planets, the sun occasionally coming between them and so forth. The boy shakes his head. "You say that nobody has found the ladder," he explains patiently. "What you have to understand is that's an argument from ignorance. Absence of evidence isn't evidence of absence. Scientists are finding all sorts of new things in our solar system all the time. Think about the asteroid belt out past Mars. That's one step along the way to Jupiter. You see, the evidence is gradually falling into place."

The girl would have every right at this point to roll her eyes. The boy's argument doesn't hold water in part because *absence of evidence often is evidence of absence*, especially when the absence comes after a long, broad and painstaking search of a limited area by many qualified investigators. In a classic Sherlock Holmes detective story, *Silver Blaze*, Holmes realizes that the key to the mystery is not the presence of something but the absence of it: nobody heard the guard dog bark. Similarly, in the case of the bacterial flagellum motor, an important clue to its origin is the absence of something after a long, assiduous search by numerous well-trained, highly motivated evolutionists—a detailed Darwinian pathway from simple ancestor to complex motor.

Is that absence meaningless? There are two ways to respond: (1) "Absence of evidence isn't evidence of absence! An unguided evolutionary pathway surely exists. Therefore, scientists eventually will discover it"; or (2) "Biologists should continue studying the bacterial flagellum motor to better understand its marvelous inner workings. But a growing body of evidence suggests that there simply is no unguided evolutionary pathway to the flagellum." The first answer illogically assumes the very question at issue. The second answer is reasonable since it follows the evidence. Nor must it stand alone. After noting that absence of evidence often does work effectively as evidence of absence, our fictional girl provided additional reasons for doubting the boy's ladder to Jupiter. Similarly, design theorists go beyond noting an absence of evidence for a Darwinian path to the flagellum motor. We also point to a common human experience. In the world around us, we encounter many complex machines that need all of their parts in order to work. Every time we can trace these machines back to their sources, we find intelligent agents. To borrow the language of the great geologist Charles Lyell, our "uniform" experience points to only one type of cause "now in operation" with the power to create new forms of such machines. The bacterial flagellum motor is a complex machine of this sort. Therefore, we have a positive reason to view intelligent design as the best explanation for its origin. Put simply, all of the available evidence suggests that this is how such machines get assembled—through intelligent design.

AN IRREDUCIBLE PICKLE

The bacterial flagellum isn't an isolated problem for the Darwinists either. The scientific literature shows a complete absence of concrete, detailed proposals for how mindless evolution could have built complex biological machines that need all of their parts to work. One of the world's leading cell biologists, Franklin Harold, opposes inferences to intelligent design. He nevertheless concedes that "there are presently no detailed Darwinian accounts of the evolution of any biochemical or cellular system, only a variety of wishful speculations."[13]

When one of us challenged Kenneth Miller with this quotation at the World Skeptics Conference,[14] Miller didn't challenge the substance of Harold's claim. He just asserted that Harold had been retired a number of years. He was implying that Harold was old and out of touch with current biological thinking and therefore could be ignored. But if Harold is so out of touch, what were the science editors at Oxford University Press thinking when they agreed to publish his recent book *The Way of the Cell?* Oxford is one of the most respected academic publishers in the world. And if Harold made the assertion out of ignorance, why didn't Miller just point to a detailed evolutionary pathway to a complex biological system to prove Harold wrong? It appears Miller didn't because none existed.

Darwinists like to claim that there is no debate over Darwinism and intelligent design within the scientific community. The reality is quite the opposite. Not only is there a debate but design theorists have the evidence on their side.

The Design Test

BIOCHEMIST MICHAEL BEHE has developed a method for spotting design in nature: look for complex systems that need all of their parts to function: common logic and common experience tell us such things were designed. In this chapter we look at how this approach can be reformulated to apply to other features of the natural world, including genetic information.

This more general method is built on longstanding methods for detecting design. Since Darwin's time many special sciences (forensic science, artificial intelligence, cryptography, archaeology, and the search for extraterrestrial intelligence or SETI) have developed an objective method for detecting design, but nobody showed how to use these techniques in a formal way for general application until Cambridge University Press published my (Dembski's) book on the subject in 1998. *The Design Inference* describes the logic of design inferences and shows how to apply it with mathematical precision.

THE DESIGN SIGNATURE

The Design Inference contains some technical mathematics and philosophy, but the heart of the book is pretty simple. When intelligent agents make things, they often leave behind a trademark or signature of design. The signature consists of two features found together: (1) the designed thing is *complex*, and (2) it fits an independently given pattern—to use the technical term, it's *specified*. The full term then for this two-part signature of design is *specified complexity*. Find either feature by itself and there's no clear indication that the thing was designed. Find them together and we have clear evidence that a mind purposefully designed the thing. Since information can possess these twin features of being complex and specified, this signature of design is also referred to as *complex specified information* (CSI).

An illustration will show that this somewhat imposing label points to a pretty commonsense way of spotting design. If we flip a coin five hundred times and write down the sequence of heads and tails, the resulting sequence will be quite complicated. We, and future generations, could spend many lifetimes trying to repeat that exact sequence at random. But despite its complexity, no sensible person would decide that this sequence of heads and tails was the result of design. Why? The sequence isn't specified. It doesn't match an independently given pattern.

Now a sequence of four coin tosses that are all heads does conform to an independently given pattern—*all heads*. So it's specified. However, no sane person would bet the farm that this series of four heads was designed (through the use of a trick coin, for instance). The reason is that the series isn't especially complex. Somebody could get four heads in a row through dumb luck probably after no more than a few minutes.

But imagine this scenario. A captured soldier appears on a live Internet video feed. His captors insist that he will be returned unharmed if his commanders meet all of their demands. The soldier is gagged and his captors train a rifle on him in case he tries to communicate with anyone watching the video. He passes the time by napping, eating gruel and flipping a quarter. He does this five hundred times and then takes a nap. Nobody pays much attention to this, until a friend of the captive, following a niggling suspicion, studies the video feed a second time. He writes down the sequence of heads and tails and discovers that the sequence spells out and repeats a message in Morse code. The heads represent the dots, and the tails the dashes. Translated, it reads, "They are holding me in the basement of the British Museum. They plan to kill me after you meet their demands."

Apparently the soldier has an all heads coin and an all tails coin (or some other way of determining the outcome). And apparently he has used this method to create a message for his rescuers. Having been presented with the Morse code message, no commander in his right mind would say, "Well, the heads and the tails were bound to occur in some sequence or other. I refuse to consider the possibility that the sequence was laid down by design." No, he would immediately infer design because the *complex* sequence conforms to an independently given pattern. In other words, the *complex* pattern is also *specified*.

Targets Wanted

Take another example, one that doesn't pass the design test. An archer blindfolds himself, spins around till he's dizzy, shoots an arrow, and then paints a target around the spot where the arrow landed so that the arrow appears in the bull's-eye. Nobody would mistake the guy for Robin Hood. And nobody would conclude that the archer had aimed for the exact spot where the arrow struck. No, everyone would realize that he imposed the pattern, the "target," after the fact. The pattern isn't independent of the arrow's trajectory. On the other hand, if a small target were set up fifty yards away and the archer nailed the bull's-eye a dozen times in a row, we would know it was not by chance. The spot the arrows hit conformed to a previously specified location. Clearly, the arrows hit the bull's-eye by design.

FAT CHANCE!

Now let's take a closer look at the other key feature used to distinguish design from chance—complexity. In detecting design, how complex is complicated enough? Would two Scrabble letters that spelled "hi" be complex enough to signal design beyond a doubt? What about "hello"? The answer begins with modern information theory's realization that we can figure how complex something is by calculating the odds of it happening by chance. The more unlikely something is, the more complex it is.

At some point a Scrabble arrangement spelling a meaningful arrangement of words becomes too long, too improbable, too complex to reasonably attribute to chance. For instance, nobody would come across a completed Scrabble game, with all of its interlocking words arranged precisely on the board and wonder whether the letters tumbled into position by chance. The arrangement is just too improbable, too complex.

To better understand the role chance plays in measuring complexity, think about a combination lock. The greater the number of possible combinations on a lock, the more complicated its internal mechanism has to be and the more unlikely it is the lock can be opened by chance. A combination lock with forty numbers on the dial that has to be turned to three specific locations in three alternating directions will have 64,000 possible combinations. (The way to calculate this is to multiply 40 x 40 x 40.) The odds of unlocking it by chance in one try then are one chance in 64,000.

Or imagine a more complicated combination lock whose dial has 100 numbers and must be turned in five alternating directions. It will have 10 billion possible combinations (100 x 100 x 100 x 100 x 100) and thus a one in ten billion chance of being opened at random on the first go. Complexity and improbability, then, are directly related. The greater the improbability, the greater the complexity. It may seem strange the first time we think about it, but the idea isn't even a controversial part of *The Design Inference*. The relationship between complexity and probability was already well established decades before in a field called information theory, a science that grew up around the invention of computers and telecommunications.[1] The founders of information theory used the improbability of a given sequence of letters or symbols to determine how complex the message or code was.

BEYOND THE REACH OF CHANCE
The question remaining is how improbable does a specified thing have to be before we can know it was designed? One chance in ten is obviously too low a threshold. One chance in a hundred is too low. How high is high enough?[2] For our purposes, we don't mind if the test occasionally misses design. We just want to make certain the test doesn't say something was designed that wasn't. That means we want to set the bar very high, meaning the thing in question will have to be extremely improbable to pass our design test.

The Design Inference sets the threshold at 1 chance in 10^{150}. Written out in long form, that's 1 chance in 1,000,000,000,000, 000,000,000,000,000,000,000,000,000,000,000,000,000,000, 000,000,000,000,000,000,000,000,000,000,000,000,000,000, 000,000,000,000,000,000,000,000 000,000,000,000,000,000, 000,000,000,000 (1 followed by 150 zeroes). Where does this

gargantuan number come from? It's based on how many tries
our universe has to accomplish something at random, such as
assembling the first living cell. The reason we need to think
about that also involves commonsense: the more tries we have,
the better our chances of managing something by chance.

Think about it on a smaller scale. If a monkey can win a prize
by randomly typing the name *George*, he doesn't have much of a
chance if he only has a few tries, since the odds of him managing
on any given try is less than once chance in 300 million. But if
he can bang away nine hours a day for a year, he has a small but
realistic chance of lucking onto the name. Nature, of course, has
a lot more to work with than one monkey and one typewriter.
We're talking about the whole universe here. Our sun is just one
of millions of stars in our galaxy. And our galaxy is just one of
millions of galaxies in the universe. A lot of purely coincidental
things can happen in a place that big.

Scientists have learned that within the known physical universe there are about 10^{80} elementary particles, that is, 1 followed by eighty zeroes. (That's big, but not infinitely big since
infinity "goes on forever," which means that infinity is infinitely
bigger than 10^{80}.)

Scientists also have learned that a change from one state of
matter to another can't happen faster than what physicists call
the *Planck time*. The Planck time is so brief it makes the blink of
an eye seem like ages by comparison. The Planck time is 1 second divided by 10^{45} (1 followed by forty-five zeroes). That's fast
but not infinitely fast. We could cram 10^{45} such transitions into
a second and no more.

Finally, scientists estimate that the universe is about fourteen
billion years old, meaning the universe itself is millions of times
younger than 10^{25} seconds. If we now assume that any physical

event in the universe requires the transition of at least one elementary particle (most events require far more, of course), then these limits on the universe suggest that the total number of events throughout cosmic history could not have exceeded 10^{80} x 10^{45} x 10^{25} = 10^{150}.

This means that any specified event whose probability is less than 1 chance in 10^{150} will remain improbable even if we let every corner and every moment of the universe roll the proverbial dice. The universe isn't big enough, fast enough or old enough to roll the dice enough times to have a realistic chance of randomly generating specified events that are this improbable.

It's worth noting here that this probability threshold is the most demanding in the literature. Cryptographers assess how secure a secret code is by imagining an attack on the system that employed all the resources available in the universe to randomly generate possible solutions to the code (even though no human code breaker could possibly martial all of the universe's resources for such an effort). Using this yardstick, they have set 1 chance in 10^{94} as the point beyond which the security of cryptosystems are safe against chance-based attacks. Computer scientist Seth Lloyd sets 10^{120} as the maximum number of bit-operations that the universe could have performed throughout its entire history. That number corresponds to a threshold of 1 in 10^{120}. Technologist Stuart Kauffman comes up with similar numbers. The French mathematician Émile Borel proposed 1 chance in 10^{50}.[3]

Each of these figures is far, far higher than what would normally be required to safely infer design. For instance, if our fictional prisoner of war had sent a Morse code signal that was only 150 coin tosses long stating twice in a row, "British Museum basement," those deciphering the message would immediately realize that the prisoner had designed the message, even though the odds of such a message occurring by chance were 1 chance in 10^{45}, an event well below the threshold set by any of the researchers noted earlier. That's because these researchers set the threshold extremely high to avoid any danger of ever identifying something as designed that wasn't designed. And *The Design Inference* set the bar even higher to be doubly sure that we avoid labeling anything as *designed* that wasn't designed.

THE DESIGN TEST IN ACTION

Now let's put the design test to work. In Darwin's time biologists thought the simplest cell was about as complicated as a tiny blob of Jell-O. This suited Darwin since his evolutionary mechanism kicked in after the first living cell that could create offspring appeared. If this first cell was simple, then its origin isn't difficult to explain. A few chemicals happen to jostle together in a certain way and presto, the origin of life. Simple.

But thanks to discoveries in the second half of the twentieth century, we now know that even the simplest bacterial cells are complex almost beyond belief. In our voyage through the cell in chapter one, we saw that DNA uses a four-letter alphabet written onto winding ladders inside the cell. These four letters are used to build the bigger alphabet of twenty amino acids used for "writing" proteins. Now if only a little information were needed for the simplest self-reproducing cell—say five or six amino acids of the right type and order—chance might do as an explanation. But in even the simplest cells, the many different kinds of essential protein machines—each tailored to a particular task—require hundreds of amino acid letters to program.

New Zealand geneticist and medical doctor Michael Denton explains it this way:

> Although the tiniest bacterial cells are incredibly small, . . . each is in effect a veritable micro-miniaturized factory containing thousands of exquisitely designed pieces of intricate molecular machinery, made up altogether of one hundred thousand million atoms, far more complicated than any machinery built by man and absolutely without parallel in the non-living world.[4]

This description also makes it clear that the simplest cell is specified, that is, it conforms to an independent pattern. In this case the pattern is that of a self-reproducing factory for producing functioning hardware and software. In our captured soldier story, it was irrational for the military commander to shrug and say "So what?" when shown the Morse code message. It's equally irrational to behold such a sophisticated factory and say, "So what? It's just a bunch of chemicals. I don't see anything here that requires explanation."

So the simplest cell is specified and pretty complicated. But is it complex enough to pass our demanding design test? In other words, is the arrangement of its parts improbable enough to exceed the 1 chance in 10^{150} threshold for inferring design? Let's take a closer look to see.

Scientists calculate that a cell with just enough parts to function in even a crude way would contain at least 250 genes and their corresponding proteins.[5] The odds of the early Earth's chemical soup randomly burping up such a microminiaturized factory are unimaginably longer than 1 chance in 10^{150}. The universe isn't big enough, fast enough or old enough to roll the proverbial dice often enough to tame an improbability that big.[6] And if the necessary string of proteins for first life did somehow appear in the primordial soup all in the same spot, it would immediately be ground into oblivion, since the protein string would lack the cell's self-directing and protective structure. Thus the primordial soup also would have to randomly generate a self-directing and protective structure for the cell at the same time and in just the right place, pushing the improbability still higher. It pushes it so high, in fact, that it stretches the ability of biochemists to calculate it. The best they can do is set a lowest possible figure, which surpasses by untold trillions of trillions of trillions of times the universal probability bound of 1 chance in 10^{150}.

At least one leading atheist, eminent British philosopher and evolution proponent Antony Flew, revisited the origin-of-life problem recently and began to rethink his position. Flew has long been held up by Darwinists as a model of incisive, rigorous and enlightened thinking. For years he insisted there was nothing in nature that should cause us to regard the apparent design in biology as real design. But after surveying the latest research into the origin of life, he has now concluded that the first life on Earth was designed. As he explained, he "had to go where the evidence leads."[7]

BIOLOGY'S INFORMATION PROBLEM

The appearance of life was a revolution in the history of matter. The ingredients of lifeless mud and the ingredients in our bodies are basically the same. The difference is in how those ingredients are arranged. How did lifeless matter first arrange itself into a living cell? In a widely cited speech Nobel Prize winner David Baltimore said, "Modern biology is a science of information." Manfred Eigen, Bernd Olaf-Küppers, John Maynard Smith and many other biologists have said that the origin of information is biology's central problem. What do they mean? A living organism is not just a lump of matter. Its ingredients are arranged in very complex and specific forms, forms chock full of information. That information poses an obvious question: Where did the information come from?

Could any purely chance process have created it? The logic of the design test outlined earlier suggests that chance alone could not produce such information.

Of course, the typical opponent of intelligent design insists that information could and did arise naturally, and they offer several possible explanations. Let's look at these strategies for explaining the origin of new biological information, one at a time.

STRATEGY 1: SPONTANEOUS GENERATION

Some claim that the first life arose by *spontaneous generation*. This means that it arose all at once without intelligent guidance. One moment it wasn't there, the next moment it was. To invoke spontaneous generation is to appeal to pure chance. The actual term *spontaneous generation* used to be quite common. In Darwin's time a lot of people believed that flies and mice formed spontaneously from rotting meat and dirty rags. And if something as intricate as a mouse could spring from a dirty rag, why not a simple cell from a warm little pond somewhere in the distant past?

The argument sounded good, but the great nineteenth-century scientist Louis Pasteur and others figured out that the flies came from eggs laid by other flies in the rotting meat. And the mice that appeared to emerge "from nowhere" were really the offspring of parent mice. Scientists no longer take seriously the idea that animals can spontaneously generate, but for a long time they went on believing in the spontaneous generation of the first one-celled organism. The reason is that they thought one-celled organisms were simple. But as we have seen, scientists now know that even the simplest self-reproducing cell is amazingly complicated, a miniature factory packed with sophisticated machines and information. Because scientists now know this, no scientist who specializes in the subject takes seriously the idea that even the first cell could have appeared by spontaneous generation.

STRATEGY 2: SELF-ORGANIZATION

Darwinism makes chance, in the form of random variations in offspring, a creative force in biology. By contrast, self-organization makes certain laws of nature the source of creativity in the origin of life. If the image of the Darwinian mechanism is a series of baby steps up a high mountain, then the image of self-organization is the sudden appearance of a whirlpool that orders a fluid and carries it downward. The whirling pattern is a case of necessity and not chance. According to the self-organizational approach, just as water under the right conditions produces a whirlpool, so the laws of physics and chemistry under the right conditions produce complex living forms, beginning with the first cell. The problem with this strategy is that all of the examples of sudden order in the nonliving world (like whirlpools) are a highly repetitive, geometric order. But the order we find in even the simplest cell is not like that. Instead, it's like the order we find in a software program or book.

Compare the following two letter sequences:

Abcdabcdabcdabcdabcdabcdabcdabcdabcdabcdabcdabcd
The fault, dear Brutus, is not in our stars, but in ourselves.

The second line is from Shakespeare's play *Julius Caesar*. It's truly complex. The first line is ordered, and it actually contains more letters than the second sequence, but it's really quite simple in its way. It's just abcd repeated, what information theorists call *compressible information*. It looks complex at first glance, but when we compress it down to its essence—repeat abcd—we see that it's simple. That's why the design test spelled out in *The Design Inference* distinguishes between such ultimately simple patterns and genuine complexity. The underlying simplicity of repetitive patterns means that they could have been caused by some repetitive, lawlike process rather than by design.

Astronomy provides a good example. Astronomers once picked up a highly regular signal from deep space. Some jumped to the conclusion that it was a radio signal designed by extraterrestrials. It turned out that the signal was created by a small, extremely dense star that sent a pulse toward Earth each time it made a full rotation. The signal was interesting but it wasn't complex in the way an English sentence is complex.

For a thing to pass the design test, it can't be the sort of pattern that can be compressed into a compact formula. It has to be complex in the way the line from *Julius Caesar* is complex.

That, as it turns out, is the kind of letter sequences we find in DNA and proteins, sequences that can't be compressed because they're nonrepetitive. And it's why self-organization theories fail to explain their origin. The laws of nature are great at producing repetitive, geometric order, but if we want to generate a long string of nonrepetitive functional information, don't call in the laws of nature. Our common experience tells us as much. Any time we find nonrepetitive, functional order—information order—and we can trace it back to its source, we never encounter lawlike forces for the cause. Instead, the source always turns out to be a creative intelligence, such as an author or programmer.

STRATEGY 3: DIVIDE AND CONQUER

Since spontaneous generation now looks like a bad candidate for generating the first life and the information it requires, origin-of-life researchers have tried to find a simpler ancestor system that might have arisen by spontaneous generation, a system that could then evolve into the first cell. If this ancestor system is too complex to have formed by spontaneous generation, then that system too will require an ancestor, which in turn may require an ancestor and so on until we get to a system crude enough to have formed by spontaneous generation. Darwin's mechanism of random variation and natural selection is biology's premier divide-and-conquer strategy. According to this model, nature takes baby steps toward greater complexity, dispensing with the variations that make the organism less fit and preserving the variations that make the organism more fit.

Darwin's mechanism is a trial-and-error approach with natural selection serving as the trial judge and random variation serving as the things on trial. If the variation is an "error," something making the organism unfit, natural selection consigns it to the evolutionary scrap heap. If the variation allows the organism to thrive and reproduce, natural selection deems it a fit stage in the process of evolution. As with all trial-and-error mechanisms, the Darwinian mechanism hinges on slow, gradual improvements. Insofar as it succeeds at all, the Darwinian mechanism succeeds by many divisions and many small conquests.

But it doesn't start working until after the first self-reproducing cell has come into existence. So it's no use in explaining the appearance of the first cell. Scientists have tried to invoke natural selection for ancestor systems before the first self-reproducing cell, but natural selection demands a self-reproducing organism to do its work. Otherwise, there are no descendants and no slight variations. All the available evidence suggests that the first self-reproducing ancestor of our living world had to be quite intricate, no matter what we call that thing.

There have been many creative attempts to push the first self-reproducing unit back to something simpler. The best known is the RNA World hypothesis. RNA molecules are used by the cell to translate DNA information into protein information. The RNA World hypothesis holds that RNA appeared first on the early Earth. It's a strange idea since RNA is the most unstable form of information in the cell. It's so unstable that usually only scientists with good hands are given the task of handling it in laboratory experiments, since it's so easy to accidentally destroy it. The unusually delicate nature of RNA makes it a poor candidate to be the one life form that sprang up in a hostile environment of nonliving matter and survived long enough to reproduce and evolve over countless generations.

But even bracketing off that serious difficulty, the RNA World hypothesis doesn't avoid the fact that even a self-reproducing RNA organism would still have to be extremely complex right from the start to have any chance of surviving and reproducing its biological information.

STRATEGY 4: MODERN DARWINISM

Many biologists concede that random variations plus natural selection cannot be invoked to address the problem of the origin of life, but they remain confident that Darwin's divide-and-conquer strategy works well in explaining the evolution of all living things after the first self-reproducing cell appeared. Give Darwinism a cell and some genetic mutations to work with, and natural selection can generate whatever new information is needed to build all of the new life forms that have arisen on

Earth, they insist. Most biologists take this as an article of faith, but their confidence is misplaced. Not only has modern Darwinism failed to explain important machines like the bacterial flagellum motor, it has failed to explain the appearance of novel biological information period.

Darwin's mechanism lacks the power to write new lines of code inside cells—the lines of DNA and amino acid letters needed to build everything from the first cells to the first mammals. Oxford biologist Richard Dawkins, perhaps the world's most famous living defender of Darwinism, insists that Darwinism is quite handy at producing biological information, but his own illustration demonstrates the opposite. To prove the power of the Darwinian mechanism, Dawkins employs a computer program that appears to gradually but randomly generate a sentence from the Shakespeare play *Hamlet:* "Methinks it is like a weasel." A six-word sentence may not seem very improbable, but grab a calculator and multiply 26 x 26 x 26 . . . , as many times as there are letters in the sentence. That's how we calculate the improbability. Everyone on the planet could dump Scrabble letters till doomsday and never randomly generate that sentence.

And yet Dawkins's random-letter-generating computer program assembles the sentence with almost magical speed. In short order it moves from nonsense to sense. What's going on here? Look inside the program and we find something rather curious. The program began with the Shakespearian line already in it, and any time the random letter generator created a matching letter, the computer seized it. In other words, the program knew where it wanted to go—it had been intelligently programmed to go there.

Despite Dawkins's eloquent protestations, this isn't how natural selection works. Natural selection doesn't have a distant goal in mind. And it can't evolve through generation upon generation of nonfunction to get to some oasis of higher function. Each generation has to be fit and functional enough to survive, reproduce and thus pass along its genetic information. The computer program obeyed no such rule. Nature may be cruel, weeding out the unfit, but Dawkins's computer program isn't. Most of the steps in the program's path from twenty-three letters of gibberish to one sentence of Shakespeare were themselves pure gibberish. They had no function at all. And yet they were allowed to survive and evolve into newer and equally nonfunctional strings of gibberish.

There are more sophisticated computer simulations that supposedly simulate a Darwinian evolutionary process successfully, but in all such programs the information that seems to magically evolve was actually inside the program from the first, either as a target phrase or as an intricate set of rules that do not resemble the rules in force in the biological realm.

Recent work by biologist Douglas Axe at Cambridge University provided fresh laboratory evidence for why the Darwinian mechanism cannot produce new biological form and information. DNA provides the building instructions for all of the various proteins. The many different kinds of proteins, in turn, serve as parts for cells and cellular machines. For new living forms to evolve from old ones, existing proteins have to evolve into very different kinds of proteins. Since the software language in protein machines uses twenty different amino acids, proteins are essentially information-rich machines built from a twenty-character alphabet. Now these proteins also require a sophisticated hardware system to function, but for the sake of argument, let's pretend that Darwinists don't have to account for the origin of this sophisticated hardware. What we want to know is this:

Back when new life forms were first evolving, how could a functioning protein evolve into a new kind of protein that performed a new function?

As we saw in our discussion of the bacterial flagellum motor, the evolving protein has to remain functional every step of the way, and it has to evolve in baby steps, not all at once. Does nature provide such a functional path from one kind of protein to a very different kind of protein? Axe's research suggests that nature provides no such path. Published in one of the world's leading journals of molecular biology, his work showed that functional protein sequences tend to occur in clusters. We can make a very small change to a protein, and it might still function. But if we keep monkeying with its amino acid sequence, soon the protein ceases to function. The protein form might be able to swim from one island of function to one of the nearby islands, but this cluster of islands is totally isolated from all other island clusters. That is, it's isolated from all fundamentally different kinds of functional proteins.

Axe's research provided a number for how rare functional amino acid sequences are for an important enzyme protein about 150 amino acids in length. Think of all the possible amino acid sequences for such a protein as a vast haystack of possible sequences. One out of every 10^{77} sequences is functional. The one functional sequence is the needle in the haystack. The number 10^{77} is 1 followed by 77 zeroes. How big of a haystack are we talking about here? Our galaxy contains around 100 billion stars. The visible universe contains around 100 billion galaxies. Together these 100 billion galaxies contain about 10^{77} atoms. The challenge for the Darwinian mechanism is to find the one atom-size needle in a haystack as big as the visible universe, and to do it through a blind search in a limited amount of time.

Think of this universe of nonfunctional sequences as a vast cosmic ocean teeming with sharks. The little evolving protein could try to swim to a distant cluster of islands, but not only is it swimming blindly via random mutations, it will also get eaten before it ever gets out of sight of its original cluster of islands. Introducing the sharks into the illustration makes sense because, remember, being in the water in this illustration means not having any function. Natural selection doesn't tolerate life forms that don't function. Like a shark, natural selection is pitiless. And there's simply too vast a sea of nonfunction between fundamentally different protein types for nature to make the journey one tiny step at a time. Axe's laboratory research strongly suggests that there simply is no evolutionary pathway from one cluster of functional proteins to a fundamentally different cluster of protein types.

Recently biochemist Michael Behe completed a book that subjects Darwinian evolution to empirical testing. Can natural selection working on random genetic mutations build significant amounts of new functional information, either alone or in conjunction with other natural processes? That's a far easier question to ask than it has been to test in the lab. Neo-Darwinism requires so many generations that it has been difficult to either confirm or falsify. However, scientists have overcome this problem by studying the evolution of microscopic life over many years. This empirical work forcefully demonstrates the severe limits of unguided evolution for generating new information, even over many thousands of generations. Consider one example, the E. coli bacteria:

> A normal inhabitant of the human intestinal tract, *E. coli* has also been a favorite bacterium to study in the laboratory for over a century. Its genetics and biochemistry are better understood than that of any other organism. Over

the past decade *E. coli* has been the subject of the most extensive laboratory evolution study ever conducted. Duplicating about seven times a day, the bug has been grown continuously in flasks for over thirty thousand generations. Thirty thousand generations is equivalent to about a million human-years. And what has evolution wrought?

Mostly devolution. Although some marginal details of some systems have changed, during that thirty thousand generations, the bacterium has repeatedly thrown away chunks of its genetic patrimony, including the ability to make some of the building blocks of RNA. Apparently, throwing away sophisticated but costly molecular machinery saves the bacterium energy. Nothing of remotely similar elegance has been built. The lesson of *E. coli* is that it's easier for evolution to break things than make things.[8]

In his endorsement of the book, Philip Skell, Evan Pugh Professor of Chemistry, emeritus, at Pennsylvania State University, and a member of the National Academy of Sciences, summarizes well the headache Behe's book has created for the defenders of modern evolutionary theory:

> Until the past decade and the genomics revolution, Darwin's theory rested on indirect evidence and reasonable speculation. Now, however, we have begun to scratch the surface of direct evidence, of which this book offers the best possible treatment. Though many critics won't want to admit it, The Edge of Evolution is very balanced, careful, and devastating.

STRATEGY 5: NEUTRAL EVOLUTION

Some have tried to get around the growing case against straightforward evolution by pointing to strands of information in cells that perform no apparent function. These strands of information supposedly are random trials that didn't work out, but there they are in the cell anyway. The cell apparently preserved the junk. These are called noncoding regions. Here the trial-and-error process apparently can go on unhindered by the need to function. In theory, this could provide a bridge from one kind of protein to another very different kind. It would work like this: experiment without penalty in the shark-free noncoding regions, then when a new functional protein emerges there, it leaps to a shark-free functional region and begins its role as a new kind of working protein.

There are two problems with this proposed solution. First, although processes of devolution no doubt have created "software bugs" in the realm of biological information, what the Darwinists write off as junk increasingly has turned out to perform various functions previously overlooked (more on this later). Second, even if we grant that there are vast areas of junk information in noncoding regions, this realm isn't a good place to evolve fundamentally new forms. The reason is that natural selection is crucial to the Darwinian mechanism, but in this realm, natural selection has no role.

Natural selection is what gives the evolutionary process its direction, not toward any one particular goal but rather its ability to progress toward greater function and complexity. Without natural selection, the evolving strand of biological information would change erratically with no regard for increased function. The reason is that in the realm of junk information, where any letter sequence is as good as any other, there's nothing around to prefer small mutations that would improve function in some other context. Natural selection isn't there to select. We're back to chance having to produce a complete and fundamentally different strand of functional information by chance alone. And as the research of Axe, Behe and others have shown, the odds of this are simply too long.

STRATEGY 6: PASS THE BUCK

Suppose there's a hole we have to fill. One way to do it is to dig another hole, take the dirt from it and fill the first hole. But now we have another hole to fill. Many attempts to deal with the origin of the information found in living things involve filling one hole by digging another. In other words, they pass the buck.

Perhaps the most striking instance of passing the buck is Nobel laureate Francis Crick's idea of "directed panspermia." Panspermia refers to the seeding of life from outer space. Crick appealed to the idea because he understood that life was too improbable to have arisen on Earth through blind processes.

In some accounts of panspermia, microbes hitch a ride on asteroids on their way to planets like Earth. Panspermia theories attempt to get around the problem of life's origin (though not its evolution). In Francis Crick's theory of directed panspermia, microbes don't hitch a ride on an asteroid but are instead intentionally carried by intelligent space aliens who deliberately place them on planets like Earth. The reason he invoked space aliens (rarely a good career move for a scientist) is because, as he argued, life is too fragile to survive on asteroids whizzing through deep space. Spaceships with carefully designed greenhouses are much safer.

Crick's panspermia idea passes the buck to some unknown place in the universe where life might somehow have been more likely to have arisen by purely natural forces. Life on Earth is thereby "explained," but life at some unknown location in the universe now becomes a mystery.

Passing the buck is not a solution. It attempts to explain the form and information we find in single-celled organisms by gesturing at the possibility of a solution elsewhere. It postpones rather than solves the problem because it never identifies a type of cause able to produce single-celled organisms on this or any other planet.

STRATEGY 7: COMMON FEATURES, COMMON ANCESTRY

A seventh strategy for countering the information problem is to point to the common features evident among various species, both in the living world and in the fossil record. According to this argument, the Darwinian principle of common ancestry predicts such common features, vindicating the theory of evolution.

One problem with this line of argument is that people recognized common features long before Darwin, and they attributed them to common design. Just as we find certain features cropping up again and again in the realm of human technology (e.g., wheels and axles on wagons, buggies and cars) so too we can expect an intelligent designer to reuse good design ideas in a variety of situations where they work.

But there is a more basic problem with the common ancestry explanation. Even if true, it doesn't solve the information problem plaguing modern Darwinism. The information problem isn't about how existing features or existing packets of biological information were passed on to new generations. The information problem is the question of how new biological information, and with it new biological form, arose in the first place at various stages in the history of life. We don't explain how the new stuff came to exist in the first place by discussing how it got passed along in the second, third and fourth place.

Thus, the focus on *common* features has a way of obscuring

what evolutionists most need to explain, which is the origin of *novel* features in the history of life. Take the example of humans and primates. The differences between them are huge—differences that go far beyond surface appearance.[9] There are no evolutionary accounts of how natural selection produced these new features from a series of random functional variations harnessed by natural selection. There is hand waving. There are vague just-so stories. But there is nothing approaching a detailed evolutionary pathway, much less compelling empirical evidence that any such pathway was actually followed in the history of life.

Nor does pointing to "missing link" fossils repair the situation. These are highly speculative reconstructions based on a bone here and a tooth there. And even if we accept them as genuine reconstructions, they fall far short of demonstrating common ancestry among humans and other primates.

Some might ask, Why else would there have been primates a bit closer in form to humans than currently exist? A little reflection yields an answer: If the primate body plan is a good one, and if a designer chose to work variations on it, who's to say that the designer should have had no interest in nonhuman primates with brain capacities a bit larger than today's nonhuman primates? There are untold thousands of species from various animal groups that have gone extinct since the appearance of primates, so the real surprise would be if we found no evidence of any primates somewhat closer to human form than now exists.

Another surprise would be to find no human fossils that vary dramatically from the norm, since humans are born all the time with abnormal physiologies due to genetic defects. How many "almost human" primate fossils are in fact fossils of humans with physiological abnormalities?

In this short book we have only the space to touch briefly on the case for and against the idea that humans and other primates share a common ancestor. Anyone interested in studying the issue further should read not only the case for a common ape-human ancestor but also the case against it. A good accessible argument against the idea appears in chapter eleven of *Icons of Evolution* by biologist Jonathan Wells. His response to leading Darwinists who critiqued the chapter's argument is available in an online essay, "Critics Rave Over *Icons of Evolution*: A Response to Published Reviews."[10]

In fairness, we should add that even ardent defenders of evolutionary biology tell people that primate fossils aren't the first place to go to demonstrate common ancestry in the history of life. Many would agree that the strongest evidence for common ancestry is molecular, in the realm we began in, the realm of cellular information. They argue that strands of genetic information held in common across both plant and animal groups (including instances of dysfunctional information held in common) provide powerful support for the common ancestry of all life.

Even this, however, is far from decisive. Take a favorite piece of evidence offered in favor of common ancestry, GULO, the gene that produces vitamin C but doesn't work in humans and other primates.[11] Although most mammals can make their own vitamin C using a functional GULO gene, primates can't. What happened? It appears their GULO gene is broken. Evolutionists argue that a common ancestor of today's primates evolved a broken GULO gene (a pseudogene) and then passed it on to its common descendants, including all of today's humans, chimps and other apes.

Biologists generally agree that our ancestors lost the functional GULO gene because their diets had so much vitamin C that they didn't need to synthesize it. This meant that when a genetic defect arose that compromised the ability to synthesize vitamin C, there was no survival disadvantage. Since there was no survival disadvantage, the defective gene was passed right on to future generations. Without natural selection to weed out these defects every time they arose, the genetic errors gradually increased until they completely destroyed the GULO gene's ability to synthesis vitamin C. By the same principle the pseudogene spread through the gene pool, unchecked by natural selection.

Evolutionary biologists regard these apparent remnants of the GULO genes as powerful evidence against ID and for common descent. Why would a designer smart enough to build animal life install broken gene sequences in a series of independently created animal types? They argue that the more reasonable explanation is that the GULO pseudogene evolved in a common ancestor and then was passed down. There's a problem with this line of reasoning, however—a pig problem.

Guinea pigs also lack the ability to synthesize vitamin C because of a bum GULO with many of the same "errors" found in the human GULO pseudogene. But evolutionary biologists agree that guinea pigs are only distantly related to primates. This means there are many animal types with functioning GULO genes that lie between primates and guinea pigs on the evolutionary tree of life. Actually, evolutionists can't agree on a tree of life. There are almost as many proposed trees of life as there are evolutionists. Even so, everyone agrees that if common ancestry is the case, primates have a lot of animal cousins closer to them than guinea pigs. This means that the bum GULO genes in humans and guinea pigs couldn't have come from the same far distant ancestor. Instead, the bum GULO gene, along with the "shared errors," arose at least twice. And in each case, the process of degeneration led to a very similar GULO pseudogene.

Given this, who's to say this process of degeneration didn't occur several times, the pseudogene arising independently each time in various primate types. With this as a strong possibility supported by genetic evidence in humans and guinea pigs, it doesn't make sense to invoke GULO pseudogenes as a knock-down argument for common ancestry. They're nothing of the sort. Thanks to the humble guinea pig, the argument, like the gene, doesn't work.

Notice a more general problem with arguments based on appeals to common pseudogenes. They are all cases of genetic information degenerating. They're not cases of new functional information being generated. So they miss the central question: *How is new form and information generated in the first place?*

What Forms Information?

We have looked at the seven most common strategies that opponents of intelligent design use to circumvent the challenge of specified complexity, including the information we find in even the most primitive life. Sometimes these strategies are used individually, sometimes in combination. Francis Crick, for instance, will use "passing the buck" to get life started and then Darwin's "divide and conquer" strategy to explain life's subsequent evolution. Stuart Kauffman will use "spontaneous generation" to get a simple "replicator" going, use "divide and conquer" to account for the day-to-day operations of evolution, and then invoke "self-organization" to get evolution over certain humps that "divide and conquer" cannot handle. All such strategies have uniformly failed to make headway in explaining the origin of sophisticated living things like a cell or a bacterial flagellum.

Meanwhile, there remains one and only one type of cause

that has shown itself able to create functional information like we find in cells, books and software programs—intelligent design. We know this from our uniform experience and from the design filter—a mathematically rigorous method of detecting design. Both yield the same answer.

CURRENT RESEARCH BY DESIGN THEORISTS

All of this talk about the design filter may lend the impression that the theory of intelligent design is solely about interpreting existing data. There would be nothing inherently wrong with this if it were the case, since many stories of scientific discovery consisted of studying existing data and providing a more satisfactory explanation. However, this isn't the case with the theory of intelligent design. Several design theorists are doing original research that tests the claims of both materialism and intelligent design.

For an extensive overview, go to ResearchID.org (http://researchid.org/index.php/Main_Page) and follow a few of the links. Below are four examples of current ID-based scientific research. Most of the description is pretty accessible, but a bit of it's heavy sledding for the nonscientist. For readers who've had about all the scientific detail they care for, feel free to skip to the final section of this chapter, "What's the Big Deal?" (p. 94). There we begin looking at the larger cultural implications of Darwinism and intelligent design.

- *Guillermo Gonzalez.* A Grove City College professor, Guillermo Gonzalez has published scores of peer-reviewed science articles and had his work featured on the cover of *Scientific American.* These articles do not make a case for intelligent design, but much of the data he has gathered relates either directly or indirectly to the design argument he and coauthor

Jay W. Richards make in *The Privileged Planet: How Our Place in the Cosmos Is Designed for Discovery.* Their design argument is testable; Gonzalez has been putting it to the test simply by doing what he normally does (e.g., discovering and studying planets outside our solar system; figuring out what parts of our galaxy are live candidates for containing habitable planets). He's also been encouraging aspiring scientists to pursue lines of research in the rapidly growing field of astrobiology, research that would bear directly on *The Privileged Planet*'s design argument.

- *Jonathan Wells.* Jonathan Wells has two Ph.D.s, one from Yale University and the other from University of California, Berkeley. He's the author of the book *Icons of Evolution*, which shows that the Darwinists favorite evidence for Darwinism, the "icons" they routinely trot out in introductory biology textbooks to support Darwinism, have all been discredited, not by design theorists but by mainstream evolutionists. That book is what Wells is most famous for, but it's not his greatest passion as a scientist. Wells has developed a hypothesis that, if true, could lead to dramatic advances in the prevention of cancer. The hypothesis concerns tiny barrel-shaped structures in cells called centrioles.[12] If the hypothesis is true, "nature" invented the turbine long before human engineers (see figs. 4.1 and 4.2). Wells's hypothesis is testable, but it requires a very expensive, cutting edge microscope, one so expensive that it's only available at a few major research institutions (including ones funded by U.S. tax dollars). The challenge for Wells has been finding a research partner with access to such equipment, somebody with the guts to partner with one of the best-known scientific critics of modern Darwinism. Since the Darwinian thought police have a strangle-

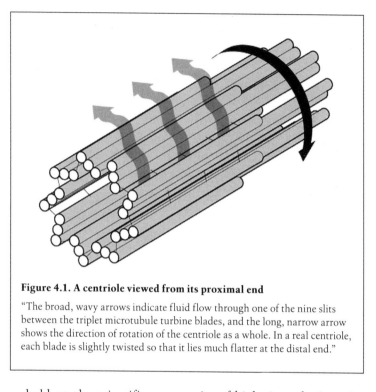

Figure 4.1. A centriole viewed from its proximal end

"The broad, wavy arrows indicate fluid flow through one of the nine slits between the triplet microtubule turbine blades, and the long, narrow arrow shows the direction of rotation of the centriole as a whole. In a real centriole, each blade is slightly twisted so that it lies much flatter at the distal end."

hold on the scientific community of biologists, that's easier said than done.

- *The Biologic Institute.* Microsoft founder Bill Gates once commented, "DNA is like a computer program but far, far more advanced than any software ever created."[13] In Redmond, Washington, just down the way from the Microsoft headquarters, is a research lab led by Douglas Axe, the biochemist we discussed earlier who got his Ph.D. at Cal Tech and did postdoctoral work at Cambridge. Axe researched protein machines and devised a way to test just how sensitive functional proteins are to tiny changes in the software code needed to create each of them. He published his findings in *The Journal of Molecular Biology*. The research that appeared there, and the research he and his Biologic colleagues are doing now, is providing increasing evidence that a mind—rather than a mindless process such as Darwinian evolution—wrote the intricate software code that makes protein machines and living cells possible. One part of the Biologic team is doing lab research on proteins. Another part, aided by a Microsoft software architect, has developed a protein folding and mutation model so sophisticated and biologically realistic that it may render everything before it quaint and obsolete. The peer-reviewed journal article describ-

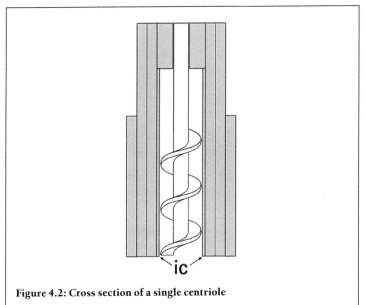

Figure 4.2: Cross section of a single centriole

"In the hypothesis proposed here, the helical structure functions as an Archimedes's screw driven by dynein molecules in the internal columns lining the wall of the lumen(ic). The rotating screw would pump fluid in from the proximal end and force it laterally outward between the turbine blades."

ing the model, and the open source code where researchers can employ the computer simulation program in their research, is available at PLoS ONE under the title "Stylus: A System for Evolutionary Experimentation Based on a Protein/Proteome Model with Non-Arbitrary Functional Constraints."

- *The Evolutionary Informatics Lab.* Founded by Robert Marks, distinguished professor of electrical and computer engineering at Baylor University, and William Dembski, this lab explores the information requirements of evolutionary processes. Evolutionary processes can be conceived of as targeted searches. If the targets are sufficiently small (as they are in biology, where the functional portions of biological configuration space are miniscule), such searches need to be given a lot of prior information if they are to succeed. In evolutionary computation (e.g., genetic algorithms) this information usually takes the form of a carefully adapted fitness landscape that determines which (virtual) organisms will be (naturally) selected. Besides doing extensive computational modeling, especially through its aptly titled "Weasel Ware" that deconstructs many inflated claims by evolutionary biologists for the power of evolution, the lab also focuses on straight mathematical foundations of information theory. Thus, Dembski and Marks have recently proven a remarkable result showing that evolutionary searches can never output more information than was first inputted.[14]

WHAT'S THE BIG DEAL?

Why do so many biologists refuse to consider design even as a possible explanation for the origin of life and new living forms like plants and animals? For some, it's simply that they were taught not to consider design as a possibility. For others, and as

National Academy of Sciences member Philip Skell argues, it's that they make no use of either Darwinism or any other origins theory in their work as experimental scientists,[15] so they simply accede to the dominant origins theory in biology—Darwinism—so they can get back to their experimental work without being hassled by the Darwinian thought police who will attack them if they step out of line (more on this later).

But what about the Darwinian thought police themselves, the zealous defenders of Darwinism who spit fire at the merest mention of intelligent design? Many of these admit that they don't like where intelligent design could lead. And they like what Darwinism does to support their own philosophy of life. This should surprise no one. Although Darwinism and intelligent design are both based on physical evidence and standard methods of scientific reasoning, both also have profound implications beyond science. We turn to this subject in chapter five.

The Poison of Materialism

THINK ABOUT HOW THE WORLD has changed in the last fifty years. A lot of good things have happened in those fifty years. Technology has improved. The United States has gotten rid of laws that treated minorities unfairly. And democracy has come to places like India and Eastern Europe.

But there also have been worrisome trends, signs of cultural decay recognized by people at various points on the political spectrum. The title of a 1993 essay by Democratic Senator Daniel Patrick Moynihan put it succinctly: "Defining Deviancy Down: How We've Become Accustomed to Alarming Levels of Crime and Destructive Behavior."[1] Should this surprise us? We live in an age when a growing number of self-proclaimed experts are telling us that "sin" is an old-fashioned idea held over from the Middle Ages, that we are not really responsible for our "bad" behavior, and that we need to rethink our entire moral code in light of modern scientific discoveries. What happened to Western culture?

POISON PILL

Ideas have consequences. And a destructive idea invaded the twentieth century, a philosophy called materialism or naturalism. Its central claim is a simple one: physical matter is all that matters, is all there is, ever was or ever will be.

For the materialist, nature has to be able to create everything on its own. Some totally natural process, not a personal God, must be the creator because matter is *the* ultimate reality. Already by the mid-1800s, there was a strong impulse among many intellectuals to see everything in purely naturalistic terms. But one thing resisted that trend: life. Things like the eye or the hand look like they are designed to perform functions. They look like marvels of engineering. Even today, atheists like Oxford biologist Richard Dawkins concede that living things look as if they were designed. How could these marvels be the product of chance or of blind forces like the chemical bonds between elements? For a long time, atheists lacked a compelling answer.

All of this changed when Charles Darwin published *The Origin of Species* in 1859. There Darwin argued that all life evolved from a one-celled organism by a simple, impersonal process. The idea that all life forms around us were descendants of a common ancestor was not new, but Darwin was the first to offer a credible mechanism, a force he called natural selection. If we have a population of organisms, there will be some variation among them. Every so often, that variation will produce a member with some survival advantage. Maybe it will fly slightly higher or run slightly faster. This creature will have a better chance of surviving, reproducing and passing on its new trait to future generations. Darwin argued that this process of natural selection working on random variations produced all the species on Earth. All it needed was millions of tiny steps over millions of generations. That's Darwin's theory in a nutshell: natural selection plus random variation does the work of a designer.

Now biologists who wanted to explain life without appealing to a designer had a way to do it. For many, this seemed to put

God out of a job. For many more, it did away with the need to believe in God at all.

OF THE PIECES, BY THE PIECES, FOR THE PIECES

By undermining belief in God, materialism undercut our view of humans as well. According to materialism, humans aren't made in the image of God. At bottom, humans are just a collection of atoms, a messy bundle of instincts and urges without higher purpose or significance. Ideas like free will, personal responsibility and even the intrinsic value of human life have no place in a materialistic worldview. That's one reason many paintings and works of literature in the modern age are full of despair. The artists aren't kidding themselves about their worldview. They're working out the real consequences of a universe without God.

Within a generation after Darwin's death, materialism and its denial of free will found its way into the American legal system. Clarence Darrow defended the teaching of Darwinism in the public schools in the famous Scopes Monkey Trial. But in an earlier case, the 1924 Leopold and Loeb trial, Darrow used Darwinism in his defense of a pair of child-murderers. There he argued that the murderers were victims of their violent evolutionary heritage:

> Nature is strong and she is pitiless. She works in her own mysterious way, and we are her victims. We have not much to do with it ourselves. Nature takes this job in hand, and we play our parts. In the words of old Omar Khayyam, we are only
>
> > Impotent pieces in the game He plays
> > Upon this checkerboard of nights and days,
> > Hither and thither moves, and checks, and slays,
> > And one by one back in the closet lays.

What had this boy to do with it? He was not his own
father; he was not his own mother. . . . All of this was
handed to him. He did not surround himself with govern-
esses and wealth. And yet he is to be compelled to pay.[2]

If DNA is destiny, Darrow is right: The murderer is no more
to blame than is an impotent piece in a losing game of checkers.
And if no one is guilty, no one is punished. The justice system is
reduced to a system of therapy and restraint, an asylum *of* impotent pieces administered *by* impotent pieces, and none to fly
over the cuckoo's nest (that is, the insane asylum) because there
is nothing over the asylum, no realm of spirit, of good and evil,
transcending the shuffle of DNA.

IMBECILES

Even more far-reaching is the legal opinion of a U.S. Supreme
Court Justice. Oliver Wendell Holmes believed that since modern science, including Darwinism, had overthrown traditional
religious belief, lawmakers and judges should decide cases
strictly based on what would have the best practical results, apparently with people like Holmes being the best judges of what
best is. Holmes also believed that society had to institute artificial selection in order to make up for the diminished role of
natural selection in modern society, diminished by modern
medicine. If that meant making it legal to sterilize people who
might be mentally handicapped, so be it. Indeed, Holmes argued for "restricting propagation by the undesirables and putting to death infants that didn't pass the examination."[3] In 1927
Holmes had an opportunity to put such thinking into practice
when the high court heard the case of *Buck v. Bell*.

Carrie Buck's mother had been classified as "feebleminded,"
a loose term routinely applied to poor and minority women re-

gardless of whether they actually were mentally handicapped. Carrie was put in a foster home and became pregnant with an illegitimate child. Her foster family promptly turned Carrie over to the Virginia State Colony for Epileptics and Feebleminded. The superintendent, Dr. Albert Sidney Priddy, asserted that she was "incorrigible" and fit Virginia's legal definition of "feebleminded." Claiming that the girl's mother had also been sexually immoral and dimwitted, he argued that Carrie was a genetic threat to society. He moved to have her sterilized under a 1924 Virginia statute calling for the mandatory sterilization of the mentally handicapped in order to improve the gene pool of future generations. The order came to sterilize, but rather than agreeing to the decision like a dimwitted little sheep, Carrie Buck fought the decision all the way to the Supreme Court. Unfortunately for her, Oliver Wendell Holmes and the Supreme Court decided against her in an 8-1 decision.

Chief Justice Holmes penned the majority decision:

> We have seen more than once that the public welfare may call upon the best citizens for their lives. It would be strange if it could not call upon those who already sap the strength of the State for these lesser sacrifices, often not felt to be such by those concerned, in order to prevent our being swamped with incompetence. It is better for all the world, if instead of waiting to execute degenerate offspring for crime, or to let them starve for their imbecility, society can prevent those who are manifestly unfit from continuing their kind. The principle that sustains compulsory vaccination is broad enough to cover cutting the Fallopian tubes. . . . Three generations of imbeciles are enough.[4]

The state sterilized Carrie on October 19, 1927. She later

married and served a productive life helping others. She loved to read, wrote letters and was active in her Methodist church. At the time of her death in the 1980s, she was not considered mentally handicapped.[5] Her daughter, Vivian, who was also sterilized, went to school for two years and was even on the honor roll at one point. She died when she was eight. It later came to light that Carrie had become pregnant not because she was promiscuous but because her foster mother's nephew raped her. If so, she may have been charged with promiscuity and committed to the institution simply to save her foster family's reputation. If she proved "incorrigible" after such treatment, it's little wonder.

EUGENICS IN AMERICA

The tragic case of Carrie Buck is no isolated incident. From the early 1900s to 1958, more than sixty thousand Americans were judged to be of inferior stock and involuntarily sterilized.[6] Minorities and the poor were special targets, and many of the victims would not be considered mentally handicapped today.

What is wrong with this picture? The United States was founded on the idea that every human being is made in the image of God and possesses basic human rights. Americans fought a Civil War in the 1860s in part to extend these rights to slaves in the South, with the leading defenders of their freedom appealing to the biblical ideas that God created every human in his image and loves people of every race and nation. A half a century later, Americans peacefully fought for and achieved the right for women to vote, again with many appealing to the biblical teaching that God made all humans, both male and female, in his image, rational creatures fully able to participate in the democratic process. And yet this same nation, a pioneer of human rights, forced both men and women onto operating tables to sterilize them.

Imagine you are a minority youth whose family receives government assistance during the 1930s. A social worker visits you, and gives you a test. You're anxious throughout the test and have trouble concentrating. The social worker classifies you as feebleminded and sends you to an institution. Once there, the doctor tells you there's a way out. All you have to do is agree to a simple operation for your health. What kind of operation, you want to know. Nobody will give you a straight answer. You are bound and carried to an operating table. An ether mask is forced over your face. There on the table you are sterilized.

It sounds like a scene out of a lurid science fiction novel. But that was reality for thousands of Americans, thanks to the eugenics movement. Eugenics has its roots in Darwin's theory of evolution.

THE DESCENT OF MAN

In Darwin's second big book on evolutionary theory, *The Descent of Man*, he issued a dire warning about how modern society was undermining his law of natural selection by helping the poor, caring for the sick and vaccinating people against smallpox:

> No one who has attended to the breeding of domestic animals will doubt that this must be highly injurious to the race of man. It is surprising how soon a want of care, or care wrongly directed, leads to the degeneration of a domestic race; but excepting in the case of man himself, hardly any one is so ignorant as to allow his worst animals to breed.[7]

After insisting that we were destroying our race by helping

the weak, Darwin pulled back and suggested we couldn't act otherwise because it would violate human sympathy.[8] Darwin's followers were not so timid. Since human technology and human compassion had largely circumvented the invaluable work of natural selection in human populations, eugenicists—including the leading evolutionary biologists of the day—set out to weed out the "bad stock" and encourage increased breeding of the "best stock."

Darwinian materialism prepared the ground for the eugenics movement in other ways. First, materialism denies the idea that humans are responsible for their choices. It insists that our decisions are ultimately the product of natural forces. Under Darwinian materialism the force that usually gets the most credit or blame is our inherited traits, since that's where Darwinism focuses attention. Thus, if someone is "incorrigible," a Darwinist like Justice Oliver Wendell Holmes would tend to assume that he or she inherited the trait and probably would pass it on if allowed to breed.

MEN AS GOD

But isn't it simply wrong to seize people and sterilize them, to treat them like cattle? Once again, materialism steps in and clears the path. Sin makes sense so long as there is a good God whose very nature defines goodness. To choose the opposite of good is to do evil, to sin. But what if there is no good God to serve as the standard of true goodness? Then we must define good and evil ourselves. And if we must define it, we can redefine it: Seizing a D student and sterilizing him or her used to be considered evil, but now we are going to define that as good and define the opposite opinion as old-fashioned. Partially delivering a baby and then puncturing its skull and sucking its brains out used to be considered an almost unimaginably hideous form of murder, but now we are going to call it "intact dilation and extraction" and define it as a good done for the health of the mother, even where the health of the mother merely refers to the woman's desire not to be physically and emotionally burdened with an unwanted baby.

The *Buck v. Bell* decision wasn't an isolated legal decision any more than the sterilization of Carrie Buck was an isolated sterilization. Since that time, judges shaped by Darwinism and materialism have taken it on themselves to redefine both the United States Constitution and morality itself.

Some are astonished at the way these judges trample on the Constitution and common wisdom. But the behavior of these judges follows logically from a materialistic worldview: if God is fallen from heaven onto the ash heap of history, then we must become our own gods.

Atheist Daniel Dennett observed, "Darwin's idea had been born as an answer to questions in biology, but it threatened to leak out, offering answers—welcome or not—to questions in cosmology (going in one direction) and psychology (going in the other direction)."[9] By the beginning of the present century, the poison of Darwinian materialism had spread from high to popular culture. Now Sprite commercials tell us to obey our thirst. Songs urge us to do it like the animals because, well, that's all we are: animals. And therapists tell us to follow our bliss, even if that means dumping our spouses and children and running off with whomever, all because, in a world without God, each of us should define for ourselves what is good and right, and let others do the same.

A BRAVE NEW WASTELAND
Materialism has been especially hard on the arts. Think about

some of the great works of art—the poems, paintings and operas, the great novels like *Robinson Crusoe*, *Pride and Prejudice* or *The Lord of the Rings*. They probe the world of flesh and blood, but at the same time they draw us into things spiritual: the sublime and the ridiculous; love, heroism and envy; good and evil.

Unfortunately, the modern world has fallen prey to an idea that says none of these immaterial things are part of basic reality. On this view, Shakespeare, Michelangelo and Mozart are in essence just so many particles bumping around, and their ideas are ultimately just patterns of neurons firing in their brains. If art reaches toward a higher plane, then it reaches toward an illusion since matter and energy are the only fundamental reality. So goes the story of materialism.

As Harvard evolutionist Edward O. Wilson explains, the human mind is just a byproduct of the brain, and the brain is just "the product of genetic evolution by natural selection." He adds, "The social scientists and humanistic scholars, not omitting theologians, will eventually have to concede that" materialism will reshape everything they study. In other words, they'll have to admit that the immortal human soul doesn't exist.

The artist fares no better in Wilson's brave new world of Darwinian materialism. The "sensuous hues" of art "have been produced by the genetic evolution of our nervous and sensory tissues," he writes. "To treat them as other than objects of biological inquiry is simply to aim too low."[10]

Wilson is implying that his approach is nobler. But treating art as a mere byproduct of Darwinian evolution doesn't lead to a nobler understanding of art. It undermines the very foundation for saying anything is noble or low or wicked.

If Darwinian materialism is right, some of our ancestors had an evolutionary mutation that caused them to imagine there's a spiritual dimension and that things like nobility actually exist. Since the illusion made them better at surviving and reproducing, the mutation passed from one generation to the next in a growing population of deluded ancestors. These creatures then worked out their delusion in everything from religion to art. So goes the story of Darwinian materialism. Materialism doesn't ennoble art. It leads people to view the very idea of nobility as a mirage. Materialism impoverishes the world and it impoverishes art.

True, there were great artists in the twentieth century who bought into Darwinian materialism. But they created original art by dramatizing how meaningless life is for those who accept that matter is all there is. The great artists of the twentieth century were everything from committed Christians to committed atheists. Some, like the poet T. S. Eliot, began their careers as skeptics and finished them as faithful Christians. But what they often wrote about was a culture in which God was at least believed to be dead. Eliot's most famous poem is "The Wasteland." Its subject isn't a physical wasteland. Its subject is the wasteland that was European culture after World War I, a culture that had cut itself off from its spiritual roots.

What are the roots that clutch, what branches grow
Out of this stony rubbish? Son of man,
You cannot say, or guess, for you know only
A heap of broken images, where the sun beats,
And the dead tree gives no shelter, the cricket no relief,
And the dry stone no sound of water.[11]

What T. S. Eliot captured in poetry the novelist Aldous Huxley captured through science fiction satire. The title of his novel *Brave New World* is taken from a line from Shakespeare's comedy *The Tempest*. Miranda grew up on a desert island and has never seen another human besides her father. That is until one day the survivors of a shipwreck arrive. Upon seeing them for the first time she exclaims, "O brave new world that has such people in it." The allusion to Shakespeare is ironic, since in the brave new world of Huxley's novel, wonder is replaced with apathy, love with drugs, and creativity with conformity. Poverty and war are things of the past. People are healthy and carefree, and technology provides unparalleled opportunities for distraction. The only problem is that to achieve all of this, society did away with the family, natural child bearing, art, literature, religion—in short, just about everything but the pursuit of short-term pleasure. People spend their spare time taking soma, a drug that erases pain and unsettling memories, and replaces them with vivid and pleasurable hallucinations. There's plenty of sex, often in the form of orgies, but little if any love. The society is a pleasure machine for pleasure machines. People have sacrificed their freedom and dignity, have given up any notion of being creatures of infinite worth, made in the image of God, and exchanged it for a series of passing pleasures on the way to the grave.

If all of this sounds vaguely familiar, it's because Huxley wrote about what he saw emerging around him, a Western society increasingly infatuated with stuff, with the pleasure principle and increasingly disconnected from history, the arts, religion—everything that probes the spiritual dimension of life. This should not surprise us. Materialism robs humans of their souls.

FROM DARWIN TO DEATH

In much of Western Europe and the United States, Darwinian materialism has drawn us toward a brave new world of trivial hedonism. It led down a more obviously nightmarish path in

Germany. And there's clear evidence of it beginning in Darwin's own writing. We saw where Darwin bemoaned that "the weak members of civilised societies propagate their kind," calling it "highly injurious to the race of man." Consider also a letter he wrote to William Graham dated July 3, 1881:

> I could show fight on natural selection having done and doing more for the progress of civilization than you seem inclined to admit. Remember what risk the nations of Europe ran, not so many centuries ago, of being overwhelmed by the Turk, and how ridiculous such an idea now is! The more civilized so-called Caucasian races have beaten the Turkish hollow in the struggle for existence. Looking to the world at no very distant date, what an endless number of the lower races will have been eliminated by the higher civilized races throughout the world.[12]

As he put it in *The Descent of Man*: "At some future period, not very distant as measured by centuries, the civilised races of man will almost certainly exterminate and replace throughout the world the savage races."[13] In *Origin of Species* he celebrates the law that says "Let the strongest live and the weakest die," assuring the reader that "from the war of nature, from famine and death, the most exalted object which we are capable of conceiving, namely, the production of the higher animals, directly follows."[14]

Separate and apart from what Darwin may or may not have intended by these words, it's a point of historical fact that some took this as a prescription for genocide. In the 1920s and 1930s, Adolf Hitler seduced Germany with the idea that they were the master race, and that they had a mandate from nature to weed out the inferior races and rule the world. He believed that one could make the world a better place by the strong weeding out the weak. He took the idea from Charles Darwin. This isn't to say that Darwin was a proto-Nazi, or that he would have approved of Hitler's attempt to conquer the world and wipe out the Jews. Nor is it to say that Darwinism led inevitably to the Nazi party or the Holocaust. But as historian Richard Weikart documents in his book *From Darwin to Hitler*, Darwinism was a pervasive influence on the development of Nazi ideology. "Without Darwinism, especially in its social Darwinist and eugenics permutations," Weikart concludes, "neither Hitler nor his Nazi followers would have had the necessary scientific underpinnings to convince themselves and their collaborators that one of the world's greatest atrocities was really morally praiseworthy."[15]

Darwinism poisoned both Nazi Germany and Europe as a whole, a point Edward T. Oakes stresses in his discussion of Weikart's book: "Darwin's theory of evolution by natural selection released a veritable Pandora's box of evil vapors and demonic spirits, which, once unleashed on an eager European public, poisoned discourse on war, race, sex, nationality, diplomacy, colonization, economy, and anthropology—especially, it would seem, in Germany." Oakes continues:

> In a letter he wrote to the German Wilhelm Pryor in 1868, Darwin averred that "the support which I receive from Germany is my chief ground for hoping that our views will ultimately prevail," a line that could well serve as the epigraph to Weikart's riveting tale of how Germany led itself (and thereby the rest of the world) into the abyss of internecine war and savagely applied eugenics, naïvely thinking all the while that it was helping to produce Darwin's "higher animal" from his eagerly anticipated "war of nature."[16]

In reading Weikart's book and reviewing the facts of history, what is striking isn't that evil was done in the name of Darwinism. Every influential worldview in history has been co-opted for evil purposes. What is striking is how reasonably and logically many of the horrors documented in Weikart's book follow from Darwinian principles.

THE AIR WE BREATHE

If naturalism was confined to the odd village atheist, it would have little impact on our culture. But these village atheists have grown far more numerous since Darwin published his theory of evolution a century and a half ago, and these atheists have worked hard to rebuild every aspect of our culture on the foundation of materialism.

We could fill a chapter with examples of modern literature and art house films that deny the existence of God, but one example from popular culture will show just how far their efforts have reached. Consider the popular Berenstain Bears series of children's picture books. What could be more innocent than these, or more wholesome than the one titled *A Nature Walk Through Bear Country?* If it were a movie, it would easily get a G rating, and yet it offers children this little nugget: "Nature is all there is, ever was, or ever will be." The line echoes the one astronomer Carl Sagan delivered at the beginning of every episode of his popular *Cosmos* television series in the 1980s: "The Cosmos is all that is, or ever was, or ever will be." Both Carl Sagan and the Berenstain Bears were stating an untestable assumption, but each presented it as established fact to a popular audience. This is the dogma, the poison, of materialism.

We see the philosophy at work whenever the mysteries of the

Christian faith are ridiculed on The Discovery Channel. We see it whenever a PBS nature program credits nature for some object of wonder instead of God. We see it whenever psychologists claim to have gotten to the root of our problems without ever considering the possibility that plain, old-fashioned sin is at the root of the matter.

Within Western culture, materialism has become the default position for all serious inquiry. From biblical studies to law to education to science to the arts, inquiry is allowed to proceed only under the assumption that nature is self-contained. It doesn't require that people deny God's existence. God could, after all, have created the world to be self-contained. Nonetheless, for the sake of inquiry we are required to approach our professional work as if God does not exist. This is the accommodating form of materialism, methodological materialism. It affirms not so much that God does not exist as that God need not exist. Its message is not that God is dead but rather that God is absent. And because God is absent, intellectual honesty demands that we get about our work without invoking him. This is the received wisdom.

Thus we see that the controversy between Darwinism and intelligent design is not an irrelevant academic quarrel over fossils and microscopic motors. The question *Where did the order of the world come from?* is one of the most important questions we can ask. Those who do not discern the action of a creative intelligence in nature imagine that the world is self-contained, self-sufficient, self-explanatory, self-ordering. Nature is God. They are God. Materialism is the idolatry of the modern mind.

In chapter six we turn to two basic strategies for responding to materialism. One sees faith and reason as occupying separate spheres. The other sees faith and reason as interrelated and reinforcing. One believes nature is largely silent on matters of faith. The other insists that scientific theories have implications for philosophy and religion. One seeks to accommodate Darwinism. The other sees Darwinism as a crucial part of the problem.

6

Breaking the Spell
of Materialism

IN THE CHRONICLES OF NARNIA, C. S. Lewis tells the story of two children and a "Marsh-wiggle" who travel deep into a series of underground caverns to rescue the prince of Narnia. Eventually they find a knight who is friendly toward them. The knight explains to them that the ruler of this underworld is a wonderful queen worthy of devotion, and that the underworld is a fine place to live. But he also warns them that every night he falls under an evil spell that causes him to rave. He reassures them, however, that every evening the good queen binds him to a silver chair so that he won't hurt himself or others when the madness descends on him.

Eventually the three travelers learn that the reality is quite different. The knight is under the evil queen's spell during the day. The spell only lifts at night when he is bound to the silver chair. And the silver chair, far from protecting him, is the very thing that gradually reasserts the evil spell on him. At night, bound to the chair, he remembers everything. He remembers that the queen is his enemy, that he hates a life lived away from the sun and that he is son of a king, indeed he is the very prince they have come to rescue, Prince Rilian.

To free himself of the spell, someone must untie him from the chair and then he must destroy the silver chair with his sword.

C. S. Lewis was a Christian, and each of his seven fantasy novels about Narnia contain hidden allegories about good and evil, about the importance of following Christ (represented by the wise and majestic lion Aslan), and about the many snares that prevent people from following him. Lewis was an agnostic before he became a Christian, so he understood well the spell of unbelief. Under the evil spell Prince Rilian is like the man who has ceased to believe there is a God or anything beyond the material world. Both live away from the light and imagine that this is the best place to be. And both forget that they are the offspring of royalty, the one from the king of Narnia, the other from the king of the universe.

In Lewis's story, Prince Rilian needed a sharp sword to destroy the chair and break the spell. We face a similar challenge and a similar opportunity. Because science is first and foremost a tool for discovering truths about the natural world, and because the greatest truth about the natural world is that it's a deliberate work of art, science can serve as a tool to help break the spell of materialism.

The Darwinists, not surprisingly, beg to differ. Many of them insist that Darwinism is perfectly compatible with traditional religious belief. More fundamentally, they insist that attempts to invoke scientific evidence to support faith are misguided because faith and reason are separate realms that should not be muddled together. Here we will argue that both claims are false.

Some of our readers may have no interest in theological arguments against intelligent design. Some of you may want to stay focused on the scientific evidence for and against intelligent design and on what can be done to promote intellectual freedom on the issue. If that describes you, feel free to skip ahead to chapter seven.

But for those curious about the theological implications of intelligent design, and for those curious about how methodological materialists try to invoke theology to place intelligent design beyond the pale, read on.

THEISTIC DARWINISM

The theistic Darwinist says the Darwinian mechanism is the tool God used to create life. Normally this approach involves no direct input from a creator after the origin of the universe and all the way to the origin of humans. At that point a Jewish or Christian evolutionist might accommodate a creator active in human history, including the possibility of miracles, the deity of Christ and even a literal resurrection.

There's an undeniable appeal to this approach. The all-powerful Creator of the universe certainly seems up to the task of using things like natural selection to get a lot of creative work done indirectly. And by professing that God used natural selection to build all of the plants and animals around us, one can preserve a certain respectability with the evolutionary establishment in our universities and elsewhere.

The problem with this approach is that, well, there are a lot of problems with this approach. Let's look at each of them, beginning with the one that, perhaps, has the strongest theological appeal: *An all-wise, all-powerful God would have been able to fine-tune the beginning of the universe so perfectly that he wouldn't need to intervene later to create life. Only when God was ready to exalt one of the apelike species by investing it with an immortal soul did he need to intervene. In between he could just let his wonderful universe do its evolutionary thing.*

On this view, God acted directly in the origin of the universe and in the origin and history of humanity, but his perfect wisdom means that nature required no additional guidance or design in between these two important events. Anything less than a universe able to churn out life all on its own, is unworthy of a God who is both all-powerful and all-knowing. On this view, there is a good theological reason to expect only natural causes between the origin of the universe and the origin of humans. The appeal of this view for orthodox believers is that it's apparently based on two tenets of traditional Judeo-Christian theism—God's omnipotence and his unsurpassed wisdom. Howard van Till calls this view of creation "fully gifted creation."[1] We're going to put quotation marks around the term every time we use it because it implies that the more traditional view of God's creative activity involves a *deficiently* gifted creation. We think that's a mistaken notion.

First, notice that this "fully gifted creation" has a lot in common with the old watchmaker view of the Creator: God is the master craftsman who created the perfect cosmic mechanism and so has been able to just let it run without additional tinkering. Stephen Dedalus, the young narrator of James Joyce's *A Portrait of the Artist as a Young Man,* describes such a God as one who "remains within or behind or beyond or above his handiwork, invisible, refined out of existence, indifferent, paring his fingernails." But there's no compelling reason to conclude that an ideal creator should behave this way. Dedalus may have, but he was a pretty cold fish. What if the maker of heaven and earth wants to stay personally involved with his creation? What if he doesn't want to wind up the watch of the cosmos and simply leave it to crank out everything from supernovas to sunflowers? What if he doesn't want to pare his nails? What if he wants to get his hands dirty? What if his relationship to creation is more like a gardener to his garden, or a musician to his instrument, a lover to his beloved or all of these?

The watchmaker image is a useful metaphor to remind us of the many mathematical harmonies and elegant regularities of God's world. But as with all theological metaphors, the theist needs to remember its limitations and recall other metaphors that reveal other aspects of God's relationship to his world.

Some who advocate a "fully gifted creation" would object that their view of God is not of a distant designer but of one "in whom we live and move and have our being," a divinity immanent but never tinkering.[2] This formulation also runs into difficulties. It assumes that a God who is simply immanent is superior to a God who is immanent but also active in ways not reducible to mathematical regularities. This is hardly obvious, as any woman could testify whose husband is around all the time but moves through domestic life with bare mathematical regularity.

The formulation also fails to remedy a crucial inconsistency. The "fully gifted" argument makes use of an important tenet of traditional Christian theism in one part of its argument, but it requires that we ignore the same tenet in another part of the argument. This is incoherent.

Let's look at the argument more closely. Parts of it are sound, but all the parts don't fit together. According to traditional Christian theism, God invented and transcends the time in which we exist—past, present and future. The idea of God transcending time is mind-bending but biblical. In Psalm 90, Moses says that to God a day is like a thousand years and a thousand years is like a day. Elsewhere God describes himself as the "I AM." He is depicted throughout the Bible as knowing and predicting future events. In the book of Revelation, God the Son calls himself the Alpha and Omega, the beginning and the end. And in the Gospel of John, Jesus uses a surprising verb tense when he tells his listeners, "Before Abraham was born, I am!"

Like many other theists, theistic evolutionists use the idea of God being over time to explain how God could exist before the big bang, that is, before the space and time or our universe came into being. Many of these theistic evolutionists also use the idea to explain how God could know that his finely tuned new universe would one day lead to the evolution of planet Earth and a species suitable for an immortal soul made in the image of God, even if the universe appears to have a random element to it. If God is outside of time and all-knowing, he can see the past, present and future of every possible universe he might create, all in a single heavenly glance.

Fine, but here's the problem: If we're agreed that God stands over time past, present and future, why criticize the design theorists who argue that the Maker of the universe appears to have done some of his design work between the origin of the universe and the origin of humans? If God stands over past, present and future, all of his design work occurred in the eternal present of the "I Am," whether the word occurred "all at once" fourteen billion years ago or at different points throughout the history of the universe. Theistic evolutionists treat God as time bound when it suits their argument and beyond time when it suits their argument. That's faulty reasoning all of the time.

Humility cautions us against placing too much confidence in our judgments about how God ought to have done things. Some insist that God wouldn't act progressively in the history of the universe or leave physical evidence of his designing work. Often such judgments trump the physical evidence right in front of us.

Surely it's shakier to guess about what God would have done, or what he chose to reveal through nature, than simply to go to nature and see what it actually reveals. It seems to be telling us that our universe, perhaps all of reality, is one where only minds generate the aperiodic sequences that make up new functional information, not regularities such as we find in the laws and constants of physics and chemistry. And since we find evidence of such information at the dawn of life, we have good reason to conclude that mind was at work there.

BAD DESIGN

We've focused a lot on the amazingly sophisticated things we find in such places as the cellular realm. But what about things in nature that appear to have been badly designed? Theistic evolutionists credit Darwinian evolution for what they regard as poorly designed things in nature. Part of the problem with this argument is that some of their favorite examples of bad design have turned out to be clever designs the critics failed to understand. The "backward wiring" of the vertebrate eye, accused of being too messy for a tidy-minded engineer, has turned out to improve oxygen delivery over the alternative design approach.

Or consider so called "junk DNA." Instances of it now appear to have several important functions previously overlooked. They regulate the timing of DNA replication and transcription; they tag sites that need to have their genetic material rearranged; they guide RNA splicing and editing; they help chromosomes fold properly; and they regulate embryo development. This is just a partial list. Far from an example of bad design, "junk DNA" has turned out to be one more demonstration that life's information-processing systems make the best computers humans have managed to devise look like child's play. When design is allowed as a possible explanation, it can press scientific investigation to not give up too soon when certain aspects of life seem unnecessary or superfluous. A design approach can thus prod science on in new and exciting directions, much as it did at the birth of modern science.

These developments represent no small failures for modern Darwinism, which predicted that things like the backward wiring of the vertebrate eye and junk DNA would prove to be examples of "bad design" incommensurate with the idea of a wise designer engineering them. However, even if numerous cases of "bad design" turn out to have clear design reasons behind their specific architectures, we will still live in a world of death and disease, of back aches and blocked arteries. Theistic Darwinists argue that we can get God off the hook for these troubling features of the natural world by blaming them on Darwinian evolution, leaving the all-wise Creator above reproach.

One problem with this explanation is theological: an all-wise Creator may have had good reasons not to make our world a perfectly pain-free place, particularly for spiritually fallen human beings prone to self-centeredness and pride.

But there's also a logical problem. If every physical event unfolded according to a divine plan hard-wired into the universe from the beginning—one that God was able to engineer thanks to his foreknowledge—then God is every bit as responsible for the evolution of vicious diseases and nasty predators as if he had designed them directly. Theistic evolutionists cannot say that God chose the results ahead of time in one part of their argument and then turn around and argue that a random process rather than God was responsible for evolutionary problems. Or rather, they can argue both things, but not without contradicting themselves.

THE BOOK OF NATURE: BANNED

Many today insist that looking for physical evidence to support religious faith is stupid since faith and reason are two separate things that shouldn't be muddled together. An essay in *Scientific American* made this point sarcastically, poking fun at a Georgia public school textbook sticker telling students that evolution is just a theory. A committed Darwinist, the writer suggested several alternative warning stickers for a series of imaginary public school science textbooks. The one in *Creationism for Dummies* would read, "Religious belief rests on a foundation of faith. Seeking empirical evidence for support of one's faith-based beliefs therefore could be considered pointless. Or even blasphemous."[3]

Does the man have a point? Some prominent Christians in academia—like George Coyne, former director of the Vatican Observatory, the astronomical research division of the Catholic Church, and John Haught, a theology professor at Georgetown University—insist that the natural world provides no such evidence, and that it would be a problem for our faith if it did.

KIERKEGAARD ON DESIGN

Several Christian theologians have tended in this direction over the centuries. Søren Kierkegaard is probably the best known. Kierkegaard lived in the first half of the 1800s. He stressed that we enter Christianity through a leap of faith, not through scientific arguments or logical proofs. As one contemporary philosopher puts it, Kierkegaard believed

> that any such proof would undermine our freedom to choose Christianity. . . . If God could be demonstrated like a math problem, then wouldn't one have to believe in Him by force of logic? Rather than by love, by choice, by gambling one's very existence with fear and trembling on the

Unknown, the very stuff of the human spirit as described throughout the Bible?[4]

Kierkegaard emphasized the priority of special revelation in matters of faith, and the limitations of evidence from nature, while still insisting on purpose and personal agency as important categories for explaining divine action and creaturely reality. Unfortunately, these nuances are lost in some of the more sweeping dismissals of evidence for design in the natural world.

A letter to the editor of a contemporary Christian journal is a good example. The notion that nature points clearly to a designer "may actually violate an important notion of theology, which is that God hides," the writer Paul Thomas commented. He continued:

> If information were conclusively discovered in the genetic code, for example, then God would have conclusively revealed himself in nature . . . belief in God would become deterministic, a no-brainer forced upon humankind, not an act of free will. God would no longer be a lover who approaches us with a still, small voice, but rather one who forces his love on human beings, turning them into automatons.[5]

Kierkegaard was stressing that physical evidence is an insufficient basis for a living faith in the personal, triune God of the Bible. Thomas, like many of his contemporaries, has gone much further.

Before deciding if such a view holds water, it's important to be clear about what it will contain if it does. To be consistent, those who insist that God would never leave indicators of design in nature, since it would strip us of the freedom to disbelieve in him, must dispense even with design arguments based on the origin of the universe, the fine-tuning of the laws of physics and the tendency of some humans in every age to sacrifice themselves heroically, never mind natural selection's drive toward organisms optimized for self-preservation. Those who insist that God would never violate our freedom with strong indicators of design must insist that all such evidence does not point to a grand designer. They must insist that brute atheism also can nicely explain all of these features of the physical universe, all the way back to and including the origin of the universe. Why? Because according to their position, even a single thing in nature pointing clearly to design would strip us of the freedom to disbelieve in God.

The argument, then, is a very large bucket. However, it doesn't hold water. That is, strong evidence for design in nature does not compel humans to believe in God.

Consider the bacterial flagellum, the intricate little rotary engine inside living cells that we looked at in chapters two and three. The flagellum provides good evidence of design and a designer, but nowhere on the bushings of the little engine are the words "Made by Yahweh." The sophisticated architecture of the motor points to design, but it doesn't tell us the personal identity of the designer, much less compel us to a living faith in the God of the Bible.

This is obvious from instances near and far. British philosopher Antony Flew has been called the world's most influential atheist philosopher. As far back as his debates at C. S. Lewis's Socratic Club at Oxford University more than half a century ago, he argued that there simply wasn't enough evidence to believe in a Creator. But recently he investigated the argument for design in the origin of the first living cell. In the process, he left atheism behind. "It now seems to me," he said, "that the findings of more than fifty years of DNA research have provided materials for a new and enormously powerful argument to design."[6] But the evidence has only drawn Flew from atheism to belief in some unknown god who doesn't have any particular interest in humans.

Flew still rejects the God of the Bible, rejects the idea of any creator who would consign his creatures to eternal punishment or reward them with everlasting bliss. Flew only affirms what he calls the god of the philosophers, an unknown designing intelligence. The evidence in nature urged him to believe in a designer, but it did not compel him to faith in the God of the Bible.

LET'S NOT LOSE OUR HEADS

Kierkegaard sought to refocus attention on the faith that grows from risking everything in search of the ragged figure of Jesus Christ. Kierkegaard was reacting against what he saw as a dry, intellectual faith without heart and soul. But in many quarters today it's the opposite extreme that poses the danger, faith divorced from reason. The most effective response is to emphasize that the Christian walk encompasses heart, mind, soul and strength. We can guard against an arid rationalism without going to the opposite extreme, without throwing out as useless the many lights of reason.

THE "YOU NEVER KNOW" OBJECTION

Kierkegaard offered a second reason for his distaste for design arguments, one that's still around in one form or another. Kierkegaard said he would "surely not attempt to prove God's existence," for even if he began the process, he would never complete it, leaving him "constantly in suspense, lest something so terrible should suddenly happen that my bit of proof would be demolished."[7]

Kierkegaard lived two hundred years ago, but this argument was the same one used in a 2005 Pennsylvania trial about intelligent design. The school decided to briefly inform students that they could learn about an alternative theory to Darwinism, intelligent design, by consulting a book in the school library. The side suing the school for doing this argued that design arguments could prove dangerous to a student's religious faith. Since such design arguments might not pan out, or might raise unsolvable questions about things like death and suffering in the world, it would be better not to expose students to them in the classroom.

This line of reasoning overlooks a couple of things. First, recent discoveries throughout the natural sciences have rendered the case for intelligent design stronger than ever. And thanks to work in philosophy of science and information theory, many have begun to realize that design can be rigorously formulated as a scientific theory. Should students be shielded from even the barest mention of this evidence because of some imagined possible threat to the student's faith?

One thing that has kept intelligent design outside the scientific mainstream for the last 150 years is the absence of precise methods for distinguishing intelligently caused things from unintelligently caused ones. For the theory of intelligent design to be a fruitful scientific theory, scientists have to be sure they can reliably determine whether something is designed. The great seventeenth-century astronomer Johannes Kepler, for instance, thought the craters on the moon were intelligently designed by moon dwellers. We now know that the craters were formed naturally. It's this fear of falsely attributing something to design only to have it overturned later that held design back. But with precise methods for discriminating intelligently from unintelligently caused objects, scientists are now able to avoid Kepler's mistake.

We now have the analytic tools to detect intelligent causes in nature with a formal precision that renders intelligent design a fully scientific theory and distinguishes it from design arguments of the past. Some of these older arguments hastily leaped from the data of nature directly to the perfect God of the Bible. The most famous of these was propounded by William Paley in his book *Natural Theology*. Perhaps the weakest part of his book is the last chapter where he sings the praises of nature's delicate balance, and how only a good God could have arranged so happy a creation.[8] Darwin turned this argument on its head, focusing instead on the brutality of nature, and seeing anything but the hand of a beneficent deity.

Intelligent design is at once more modest and more powerful than Paley's natural theology. From observable features of the natural world, proponents of intelligent design infer to an intelligence responsible for those features. The world contains events, objects and structures that natural forces lack the power to have caused. Moreover, these things have the signature of intelligent design. This is not an argument from ignorance. Nor is this a matter of personal incredulity. Precisely because of what we know about natural causes and their limitations, and precisely because of what we know about things known to be products of intelligent design (e.g., cars and computer programs), researchers are now in a position to demonstrate design rigorously.[9]

There's an important contrast to keep in mind here. Science, we are told, studies natural causes, whereas to introduce God is to invoke supernatural causes. This is the wrong contrast. The proper contrast is between *natural causes* on the one hand,

and *intelligent causes* on the other. Intelligent causes can do things that natural causes cannot. Natural causes can fling Scrabble pieces around in a storm, but they cannot arrange the pieces to form a meaningful series of interlocking words. To obtain a meaningful arrangement of more than a few letters requires an intelligent cause. Whether an intelligent cause operates within or outside nature (that is, whether the intelligent cause is natural or supernatural) is an interesting and important question, but it is a separate question from whether an intelligent cause has operated.

The case for intelligent design shows that chance and impersonal laws do not explain the information coded into cells, do not explain the tiny living robots like the bacterial flagellum, do not explain the many body plans that suddenly appear in the fossil record during the Cambrian period, do not even account for the way the laws of nature themselves are fine-tuned for life. At the same time, our case shows that there is only one type of cause known to produce things like biological information—intelligent design.

THE HEAVENS DECLARE

Is the evidence for design in nature real, and are arguments based on that evidence soundly constructed and well informed? These are the key questions. If the signature of design in nature is authentic, who are we to insist it is a gift God shouldn't have given?

The science of intelligent design is a form of human exploration valuable in its own right: the scientist open to the truth, searching out the best explanation for some corner of the natural world and fashioning a compelling argument for design based on empirical evidence and sound reasoning. But in being all of these things first and foremost, it can also serve another function.

We live in an age where the secular institutions of the West insist that science can only consider material causes. They have closed the book of nature by insisting that researchers in virtually every field must only offers theories fully consistent with atheism. They rarely put the matter this baldly. It usually goes by the benign, official-sounding term *methodological naturalism* or *methodological materialism.* The terms are sleep-inducing, and maybe that's the idea, for materialism is a spell cast on the West, a spell potent enough that even some Christians frown disapprovingly at scientists who risk their careers to announce that they see, through today's powerful microscopes and telescopes, evidence of design.

And while some Christians imagine that faith is incompatible with indicators of design in nature, and while they rush to find some compromise that keeps faith and reason neatly separated, the psalmist proclaims from under a starry sky without qualification or apology,

The heavens declare the glory of God;
    the skies proclaim the work of his hands.
Day after day they pour forth speech. (Psalm 19:1-2)

Deeper into his hymn of praise, David moves from the generic *El* to the Creator's personal name revealed in Scripture: *Yahweh.* He makes this switch just as the subject moves from the book of nature to the book of God's written law. In this way David suggests that the evidence for design in nature can point toward a grand designer, thus putting us in a position to at least consider the case for the particular God of Scripture.

STEPPING STONES
There are people, many of them young, standing on a far shore.

They have heard of the man Jesus, but they've been told that he is just out of reach, a lovely myth, a figure from a time before reason when people believed in a white-bearded God forever tinkering with the world, trying to set it aright. The evidence for intelligent design can counter this false propaganda.

We could tell many stories of people, already in love with the figure of Jesus, who walked into a building as atheists and left as believers after seeing accomplished scientists and philosophers explaining the growing evidence for design in nature. These converts were people in the strangely modern circumstance of already knowing about Jesus, even loving him, but who had been told that nature—reality itself to modern minds—has moved beyond such childish tales. Such people do not need cautious explanations of why evidence of design would strip them of their freedom. They are in bondage already, are under the spell of materialism, and they need someone to break the spell. The evidence of intelligent design often helps do exactly this.

The Book of Nature

Lifting the Ban

ATHEIST DANIEL DENNETT described Darwinism as a "universal acid" that has fundamentally transformed every aspect of Western culture.[1] Dennett was half right. Darwin gave us a creation story, one in which God is absent and unthinking natural processes do all the work. But if Darwinism is an acid, it's also a foundation, a creation story that intellectuals have been building on for more than a hundred years. Now a growing body of evidence is undermining that foundation. When it crumbles, so too will the things built on it. But what will be built in its place? And who will do the building? The theory of intelligent design presents a golden opportunity for a new generation of scholars.

This final chapter is a how-to manual for using the investigative tools of intelligent design to reinvigorate our culture by reawakening it to the powerful evidence of design in the natural world. The chapter touches on ways for aspiring scientists to pursue research to further enhance the case for intelligent design. It offers advice on navigating the often treacherous world of research universities. It discusses ways that students who are not pursuing careers in science also can make valuable contributions. It discusses the organizations that high school and college students can join or form. And it offers advice about how parents, teachers and other citizens can defend the academic and intellectual freedom students and researchers need to follow the evidence in nature, no holds barred.

Some sections of this final chapter will apply directly to you. Others may be irrelevant to you. And some may apply to someone who values your advice. So feel free to skip around in this section. There's no cumulative argument stretching across the whole chapter that will fall apart if you jump ahead. For instance, the first section offers advice to aspiring young scientists. If you aren't one of these and have no influence over one of these, then you may want to jump to the next section where we discuss some important things others can do to help reorient our culture to the reality of design and meaning in the natural world.

TESTING DESIGN

The first thing aspiring scientists interested in the theory of intelligent design can do is put to rest the false claim that contemporary design arguments are not testable. Certainly the idea that there is a transcendent Maker beyond our universe is not a falsifiable claim (we'd have to look everywhere outside our universe for starters), but specific design arguments are falsifiable and by extension testable.

Earlier in the book we showed how biochemist Michael Behe's design argument involving molecular machines is testable. And the excellent website <www.researchid.org> lists several other testable design arguments, including several research ideas that aspiring scientists could pursue, in fields as diverse as astrophysics and cell biology.

This is important work, but we should emphasize that the call to research isn't for lack of existing evidence for intelligent design. There's already a wealth of evidence to support intelligent design. It's just that a powerful way to counter the incessant barrage of misinformation directed against ID is to direct attention to fresh experimental evidence. Doing original research also is a good way for young scientists to build a bully pulpit for their design arguments. Scientists open to the possibility of design in the natural world aren't blinded by materialistic assumptions. That means they can consider research ideas that might never occur to methodological atheists.

INTELLECTUAL FREEDOM UNDER ATTACK

Having said this, it would be irresponsible of us not to urge caution. Graduate students, and even young professors who do not have tenure, must proceed with care as they navigate the minefield of academia. We know this from painful experience. While some Darwinists welcome open discussion of the evidence, many more in positions of power have gone to great lengths to shut down open conversations about the evidence. They're waging this attack on academic freedom at taxpayer-funded universities and research facilities, private secular universities and even many Christian colleges and universities.

Such a claim may sound melodramatic, but in this case reality is melodramatic: undergraduates have been denied recommendations, graduate students have been denied Ph.D.s, and professors have been fired simply for violating the sacred dogmas of methodological atheism and modern Darwinism. The attacks on design theorists and those defending open and balanced discussions of the theory have increased both in frequency and viciousness. A story on National Public Radio provided a sobering overview, describing how leading Darwinists have sought to undermine or destroy the careers of several scientists for either defending or merely promoting discussion of intelligent design.[2]

The NPR reporter, Barbara Bradley Haggerty, noted that eighteen scientists spoke to her about such attacks, but most refused to allow their names to be used for fear they would be attacked and their careers torpedoed. As if to prove that this really is the standard operating procedure, opponents of intelligent design attacked the reporter's religious beliefs and professional ethics after the story aired, leveling a series of spurious charges without evidence.[3]

One of those who attacked the reporter, University of Minnesota-Morris evolutionist P. Z. Myers, was already on record urging his fellow ID critics to take off the gloves when it comes to dealing with people like Haggerty. "Our only problem is that we aren't martial enough, or vigorous enough, or loud enough, or angry enough," he advised. "The only appropriate responses should involve some form of righteous fury, much butt-kicking, and the public firing and humiliation of some teachers, many school board members, and vast numbers of sleazy far-right politicians."[4]

In a similar vein, intelligent design critic Liz Craig, of Kansas Citizens for Science, wrote:

> My strategy at this point is the same as it was in 1999: notify the national and local media about what's going on and portray them in the harshest light possible, as political opportunists, evangelical activists, ignoramuses, breakers of rules, unprincipled bullies, etc.

She concluded, "There may [be] no way to head off another science standards debacle, but we can sure make them look like asses as they do what they do."[5]

For those who want to see the attack on intellectual freedom with their own eyes, rent or buy the simultaneously funny and sobering documentary *Expelled: No Intelligence Allowed*, hosted by cultural commentator, actor and comedian Ben Stein.

We might assume that safety at least could be found in seemingly conservative places like Baylor University, an academically respected Southern Baptist university in Waco, Texas. But as the documentary makes clear, sometimes this isn't the case. Indeed, sometimes these are the worst places for those opposed to methodological atheism, what University of California, Berkeley, emeritus law professor Phillip Johnson refers to as MN or methodological naturalism. "Anyone who rejects MN invites conflict with the all-powerful rulers of science, whose approval is indispensable to Christian professors who want to be in the academic mainstream," Johnson explains. "The point of theistic MN is to allow theists to survive in a naturalistic academy. But if the academy is committed to naturalism, then the gulf between the academy and the sanctuary can be narrowed only to the extent that naturalism also dominates the sanctuary."[6]

Places like Baylor can therefore be even worse than ultrasecular universities like Harvard and Yale. The Ivy League universities have nothing to prove. But many professors at Christian universities (such as Baylor) or at public universities in "flyover" country (such as Iowa State) desperately want to show the Harvards and Yales of the world that "We're sophisticated and enlightened too; don't let the hick location of our university fool you."

What should defenders of academic and intellectual freedom do about this? We recommend one strategy for aspiring young scientists and another for everyone else.

PROCEED WITH CAUTION (AND SHREWDNESS AND COURAGE)
To the aspiring young scientist persuaded that evidence in nature points powerfully to intelligent design, we recommend that you let discretion be the better part of valor. Contribute to your field, get your Ph.D. and secure a position at a research institution. Pursue excellence. Ideally, wait till you have tenure. Then, when the time is right, speak clearly and boldly against the suffocating dogma of methodological atheism. Until then, keep your powder dry. Patience is not a sin. Prudence is not a sin. Shrewdness and self-discipline are virtues. In sum, keep a firm rein on the tongue while you build up your scientific credentials and expertise. The saying "loose lips sink ships" is an old, durable saying for a reason. This advice means more than not spouting off about your opinions. You may be asked questions at certain points, questions designed to sniff out scientific unorthodoxy. You need to think about how you will respond, maintaining integrity without alienating those who may hold your academic future in their hands.

Respected, established scientists who openly oppose methodological atheism are invaluable assets for cultural transformation, and we need more of them. But there won't be more of them if young graduate students fall on their swords for the cause of intelligent design.

If you're in the biological sciences and you have the time, patience, stamina and inclination, consider pursuing a medical degree first, followed by a research degree. A poll by the Finkelstein Institute found that some 60 percent of U.S. medical doctors are skeptical of the idea that the origin of humans can be explained in strictly unguided terms. The percentage is probably lower among medical school professors, but there may be medical schools where academic freedom on the question of Darwinism and design is real. And in any case, having a medical degree provides both an excellent fall back and a fine calling card in a culture that often respects the opinions of M.D. biologists more than those of Ph.D. biologists.

OPPORTUNITIES FOR THE NONSCIENTIST STUDENT

For those students not going into the sciences, and even for those in applied sciences (such as medical school), your situation may offer greater room to maneuver early on. Students outside the sciences are sometimes granted some degree of intellectual freedom on this subject. You may not win any points for openly opposing Darwinism or methodological atheism, but in many cases, you'll be tolerated, particularly if you proceed respectfully and with discretion. If you've carefully studied the lay of the land and are convinced that your academic situation is one where you can stick your head up without getting it lopped off, then one immediate, practical thing to consider doing is joining or starting an IDEA Club on your campus.

IDEA stands for "Intelligent Design Evolution Awareness." The first IDEA Center was formed in 2001 at the University of California, San Diego, and today there are chapters at universities and high schools across the country and around the world. As their website explains, the clubs are "dedicated to promoting intelligent design theory and fostering good-spirited discussion and a better understanding over intelligent design theory and the creation-evolution issue among students, educators, churches, and anyone else interested" (see www.ideacenter.org).

CITIZEN WORK

What about those who have completed their education and are not in academia? Perhaps surprisingly, here is where some of the most immediate good can be done and a good deal of immediate harm avoided. Think about it. More than 80 percent of Americans are skeptical of the idea that humans emerged from purely mindless, unguided evolution. Only about one in eight Americans in the poll said they were convinced that humans evolved through a process that God had nothing to do with.[7] The vast majority, among both the educated and uneducated, both Republicans and Democrats, are convinced that intelligent design played a role in the history of life. This sizable majority pay most of the taxes and tuition that fund our public universities, and they provide most of the donations and tuition money that funds our private universities.

This overwhelming majority should be a powerful champion for intellectual freedom against those who have made methodological atheism the nonnegotiable dogma of academia. Unfortunately, it hasn't worked out that way so far. Many methodological atheists are waging a well-orchestrated and ruthless campaign to stamp out any evidence of design, any scientific arguments for design and anyone in academia arguing that nature points to design. And in most cases, their campaign is paid for by our tax, tuition and charitable contribution dollars.

If you think there's something wrong with this picture, if you sense an untapped opportunity for good, read on. There are smart things that taxpayers committed to academic and intellectual freedom can do, and some very stupid things. In the next pages, we'll look at how to pursue the first and avoid the second.

KANSAS AND THE SILENCED MAJORITY

My (Witt's) old college town paper, the *Lawrence Journal-World*, reported in November 2005 that a new class at the University of Kansas would work to discredit the theory of intelligent design.[8]

The class, taught by religion professor Paul Mirecki, chairman of KU's religious studies department, was initially titled "Special Topics in Religion: Intelligent Design, Creationism and Other Religious Mythologies." In an e-mail to an atheist listserv, Mirecki wrote, "The fundies [fundamentalists] want it all taught in a science class, but this will be a nice slap in their big fat face by teaching it as a religious studies class under the category mythology." Mirecki later offered a tepid apology for the e-mail, noting that he didn't intend for the e-mail to end up in the public square (meaning he was mainly sorry he was caught).

Is Mirecki indicative of where the University of Kansas is headed? I don't know. When I taught at KU back in the 1990s, I received solid teacher evaluations, but I was reprimanded by the coordinator of freshman composition because two students who were earning abysmal grades complained that I was injecting religion into the classroom. How had I done this? When I taught Nathaniel Hawthorne's "Young Goodman Brown," I explained to the students the religious background of both the author and characters (Christian). When I taught Isaac Bashevis Singer, I explained the religious background (Jewish) of the author and characters. When I taught "The Open Boat" by Stephen Crane, I described philosophical materialism, the worldview that seems to be conveyed in that story. In the course of our discussions about these stories, some students asked me what my own belief system was, and I said I was a Christian. We then moved back into a discussion of the literature. For such behavior I was called into an office and reprimanded.

Fortunately, that was not representative of my experience at KU. Most of my professors, even the agnostics, I suspect would have been appalled by this reprimand. What I valued about my time as an instructor and graduate student at KU was the genuine diversity of faculty views. Unlike some universities that talk about diversity but fill all of their faculty positions with anti-Christian and anti-Jewish secular humanists, my academic work at KU brought me into contact with a broad range of worldviews, from atheists to pantheists to conservative and moderate Catholics to professors who weren't sure what they believed about ultimate things.

I fear that this KU of a previous decade may be vanishing, that the older generation of professors, many of whom held to some form of traditional theism, some of them even politically and religiously conservative or moderate, have been steadily replaced over the subsequent decade by far left-wing materialists.

This has certainly been the case at other universities, and the drift shouldn't surprise us. The radical left believes that politics is essentially about power, and that in the end everything is politics. Given such an outlook, why should they, when the balance of power tips in their favor, carefully cultivate intellectual diversity in their various academic departments? By the logic of their worldview, they shouldn't. If they think everything ultimately boils down to power, then we should expect exactly what we're seeing in modern American academia—an orchestrated effort to dominate the university landscape by any means necessary. Such behavior isn't the least bit puzzling. What's puzzling is that the voting taxpayers and the conservative politicians they elect in conservative states such as Kansas appear unable or unwilling to do anything about it.

Are they cowed by the charge that taking action would infringe on academic freedom? The reality is just the opposite: they need to take action to protect academic and intellectual freedom.

A generation ago, the student editor of the Dartmouth school newspaper let it be known that he was a political conservative.

For this he was sacked from his position. Dinesh D'Souza tells the story in *Letters to a Young Conservative*. This happened at a private university. But when things like this occur openly at tax-payer funded *public* universities in states heavily populated by conservatives and old-school liberals who still value intellectual freedom, why won't the politicians who represent them stand up and do something? We don't mean stand up and make token gestures either. There's never a shortage of those. We mean strategic and sustained efforts at reform, the sort of bold, patient, shrewd leadership that, for instance, freed Poland from the grip of communism. Maybe the comparison suggests a partial answer: such a response demands a host of personal virtues that are sometimes in short supply.

VAMPIRE MANAGEMENT 101

This is not the place for a detailed plan of action, since every family situation and every university situation is different. But a couple of *don'ts* leap to the fore, *don'ts* routinely ignored by supporters of theistic values in American culture.

A short parable will illustrate what we mean. Imagine you have a sometimes charming vampire in your neighborhood—charming but destructive. How do you deal with the fellow? Well, defeating a vampire is no easy task, but some don'ts are fairly clear. First, stop feeding him. Translated: stop sending the offending university your donations even though, gee, they have a football team you love and, heck, you met the love of your life there twenty-five years ago. While we're at it, maybe stop feeding them your children by sending them there. Vampires do bad things to young people. This is commonly understood. Universities run by academics hell-bent on applying methodological atheism to every nook and cranny of reality also frequently do bad things to young people. This is all too rarely understood.

That said, don't assume a Christian university is necessarily any safer. In some cases they can be more dangerous, since students go there thinking they've entered a safe haven. There's no substitute for doing careful research about any institution to which you're thinking of sending yourself or your kid. And careful research doesn't mean simply reading the public relations literature put out by the college. It means seeking independent and even contrarian voices. These won't necessarily provide the more accurate source, but often they will point the way to telling facts you would otherwise have missed, facts that merit closer scrutiny.

If the university you attended twenty-five years ago has changed for the worse, don't pretend everything's basically the same. And don't let a state university that has thrown academic freedom out the window get away with the usual scare tactic: "Lavishly fund us or the regional economy will collapse." If you're worried about inadequate funding for universities and colleges in the state, then encourage policies that give parents and students control. Programs like the Texas Equalization Grant program already do this to a limited degree, providing a certain amount of grant money for qualified applicants, money that can be applied to any accredited university, public or private.

Strong grassroots action combined with shrewd, focused and passionate political leadership open up ways to apply effective financial and public pressure on universities to restore real intellectual freedom and balance, and strengthen our higher education system in the process.

Some may scoff that there aren't enough smart, qualified worldview-conservatives out there to restore balance. Rubbish. The qualified people have simply tracked into other careers.

And in any case, there are plenty of possibilities moving up through the undergraduate and graduate ranks. If the academic establishment spent as much energy trying to achieve worldview balance as it does trying to achieve skin color balance, it would have the problem remedied in just a few years.

MORE LIGHT

Let's return to our sometimes charming but destructive vampire. You've stopped feeding him. What else should you do? Well, draw him into the light. Vampires don't like that a bit. The same strategy works on universities that have become propaganda machines for methodological atheism. Use every communication tool at your disposal to communicate to other citizen taxpayers what's actually happening at the university. If more people knew what their tax dollars were funding, it'd be much easier to change things for the better.

There are countless ways to shine a light. Consider one relatively easy one. If you are decent at writing concise, persuasive arguments, submit letters to the editor of your campus or local newspaper whenever an issue concerning intelligent design, Darwinism or methodological atheism arises in the university or college town paper. Find out the length requirements and format, and stick to one clear point. Most beginners make the mistake of trying to cram everything but the kitchen sink into their letters. Better to find the most important point and argue it well.

The mandarins of methodological atheism will complain that efforts to stop our tax dollars from funding attacks on academic freedom somehow violate *their* academic freedom. Nonsense.

Theirs is a curious notion of academic freedom. When it came to light that several Iowa State University professors were seeking to have astronomer Guillermo Gonzalez fired for his view that scientific evidence pointed to intelligent design, at least one protested that they were simply exercising their academic freedom to deny Gonzalez tenure. In another case, this one at Texas Tech University in Lubbock, Texas, biology professor Michael Dini followed a stated policy of denying even excellent students recommendations to medical school unless they affirmed a personal belief in human evolution, never mind their religious beliefs, never mind the cogency of their arguments for doubting human evolution, never mind that most U.S. medical doctors do not affirm modern evolution's account of human origins.[9] Many in the community urged Dini to drop the policy. Dini and his supporters responded by insisting he had the academic freedom to maintain his policy.[10]

Notice what they're saying in both cases. An academic should have the academic freedom to deny other professors and students their academic freedom, provided he's in a strong enough position to do so. Pretty slick, huh? Well, slick and oily, to be precise. That becomes obvious when you drag it into the light. The deeds of darkness love the shadows. Don't give them the shadows.

HIGH SCHOOL BIOLOGY: LEAVE THE AIRBRUSH BEHIND
Most public high school biology classes offer a decidedly one-sided view of evolutionary theory, an airbrushed portrait of that 150-year-old fellow named modern Darwinism. If students had nothing else to go on, typically they would reach the end of the evolution unit convinced that there are no weaknesses in modern evolutionary theory and no scientists, other than a few nutcases in a padded cell somewhere, are skeptical of the theory. The conviction is itself nutty, and students deserve better. There are significant weaknesses in the modern theory of evolution, and many scientists are skeptical of its claims. What should par-

ents and students do about the taxpayer-funded propaganda-fest that misleads students on this point?

First the short answer. Then the long answer.

Short answer. Don't insist that public schools teach the theory of intelligent design alongside Darwinism. Instead, push states to teach students both the strengths and weaknesses of modern evolutionary theory. In other words, encourage public schools to teach good critical thinking skills concerning modern Darwinism. Call it the strengths-and-weaknesses approach. Give students the evidence for and against evolution—all of which can be found in the mainstream, peer-reviewed scientific literature—and allow students to evaluate the data. If the theory is so powerful, if it finds overwhelming support from the evidence, then it should have nothing to fear from balanced, critical analysis.

If it's a private school, encourage them to expose students to the case for intelligent design alongside the case for modern Darwinism. ID is perfectly scientific and, as we argue in this book, strongly supported by the evidence. A good textbook for private- and home-school biology classes recently appeared, with me (Dembski) as one of the editors: *The Design of Life*, coauthored by biologist and *Icons of Evolution* author Jonathan Wells. If you can't get any traction on this proposal, encourage them to at least teach the strengths and weaknesses of evolutionary theory.

The long answer (with the focus again on the public school situation). There is nothing unconstitutional about teaching public school students about the evidence for intelligent design. According to the Supreme Court, school policies must fulfill a legitimate secular purpose to be constitutional. Teaching students about the scientific data and arguments relating to intelligent design ought to meet that standard. It's particularly ludicrous to contend otherwise in cases where students would also be hearing the evidence for theories that claim to refute intelligent design, such as modern Darwinism.[11] However, well-funded groups like the American Civil Liberties Union (ACLU) and Americans United for the Separation of Church and State are dedicated to driving even the faintest hint of intelligent design from the public square. This means that even a proposal as modest as exposing kids to the evidence for design in nature will be met with an extremely well-funded and well-orchestrated campaign to mischaracterize it and then stomp it into oblivion.

This is what occurred in Dover, Pennsylvania, in 2005. The local board of education wanted to give students some inkling that not every scientist, not every piece of evidence, supports modern Darwinism, so they called for a short statement at the beginning of the biology unit on evolution informing students about an alternative theory of biological origins, intelligent design. The statement told students that if they wanted to learn more about it, they could find a book on the subject in the school library.

Pretty benign, right? Yes and no. It certainly should not be considered illegal, but America's activist judiciary doesn't always do the obvious or reasonable thing. The policy was timid enough to do the students little real good but clumsy enough to put the school in real legal danger. It did not help that the school board members themselves seemed confused as to what intelligent design is, and at least some board members may not have had secular reasons for supporting the policy. The Discovery Institute's Center for Science and Culture urged the school board to scrap the policy before it was sued. Since the leading proponents of intelligent design are fellows of Discovery Institute, one would think the warning would have given the school board pause. But the well-meaning board ignored the advice. The Discovery Institute encouraged them to pursue a strategy that was both safer and more substantive (the strengths-and-weaknesses strategy), but the school board wanted to go for the Hail Mary, as did the legal team they hired to represent them.

Hail Mary passes make sense when time is running out in a football game and there are no other options. But time isn't running out. The evidence for intelligent design continues to accumulate, and more and more scientists are expressing skepticism toward modern evolutionary theory. Patience, not panic, is the order of the day. In the case of the Dover trial, the Dover school board's clumsy Hail Mary pass, like most Hail Mary passes, was batted away.

The judge's idea of good background research for the case was to watch a fictional Hollywood dramatization of the 1925 Scopes Monkey evolution trial. The old Hollywood movie changed several key facts from the actual court trial in order to paint the pro-evolution forces as angels of light and their opponents as unalloyed forces of reaction, idiocy and darkness. Judge Jones told a reporter for *The Philadelphia Inquirer* that he planned to watch the movie to provide "historical context,"[12] never mind that a well-known Pulitzer Prize-winning book written by a Darwin defender forcefully details the many gross and misleading historical errors in the film.[13] Not surprisingly, given his research tastes, Judge Jones eventually ruled against the school board for instructing teachers to note the alternative theory and the ID library book to students. Briefly mentioning intelligent design as an alternative to Darwinian evolution amounted to the establishment of a religion, he argued.

He was praised by the pro-Darwin media as a brilliant, independent judge who swam upstream against political pressure, never mind that he attended a decidedly pro-Darwin church and became the toast of the national liberal media afterward. And never mind that he cut and pasted the vast majority of his analysis of ID directly from a document drafted by attorneys working with the ACLU. This goes some way to explaining why there were easily checkable factual errors in his written opinion, such as the false claim that there were no peer-reviewed science papers written by design theorists supporting intelligent design.[14] Judge Jones apparently didn't even read the briefs submitted to him on the intelligent design side of the trial. He just took the word of the lawyers working with the ACLU and delivered an opinion that made them proud of him. Fortunately, high-level scientific disputes aren't settled by low-level district judges.

OPINION AS CLUB

Judge Jones's opinion has no jurisdiction outside the small Pennsylvania district, but it was later used effectively to scare Ohio State Board of Education members to back away from a more modest policy advocated by Discovery Institute, one that has never encountered legal trouble, namely the policy of teaching students the strengths and weaknesses of modern evolutionary theory and permitting rather than mandating voluntary discussion of intelligent design when a student raises a question about it.

The Darwinists later used a similar tactic to scuttle a similar strengths-and-weaknesses approach in Kansas, but with a twist. Here the citizens had voted into office a school board that tilted in favor of teaching the strengths and weaknesses of evolutionary theory, and with help from Discovery Institute scientists and legal experts, they pushed through a recommended policy in 2005 that called for just such an approach in the state's public high school biology classes. In response, the Darwinists revved up their scare campaign, threatening lawsuits and the end of Western civilization as we know it if students were exposed to evidence against Darwinism.

But they did one other thing too. They helped fund and promote the campaigns of Darwin-only state school board candidates in the Republican primaries of a nonpresidential election year, elections that typically have low voter turnout. A lot of citizens firmly opposed to a Darwin-only approach never made it to the polls, while the Darwin-only people beat the bushes and got sufficient turnout to push their candidates through. Many of those opposed to the Darwin-only approach hardly knew what hit them. Many probably thought the real political fight would come in the general election where the Republican candidate would face off against a Darwin-only Democratic candidate. But the battle was already over by the time the general election arrived.

This was apparently a case of methodological atheists caring more about what went on in our public schools than the majority of Kansas citizens who view Darwinism as false and injurious.

The cases of Dover, Ohio and Kansas suggest three things for future efforts to bring balance to the way students are taught evolution in public schools. One, if you're skeptical of modern Darwinism, consider the advice of the design theorists who have been involved in this academic freedom effort from the beginning. They have learned many valuable lessons from hard experience. An excellent website describing what has worked and what hasn't worked is located at the Center for Science & Culture website (www.discovery.org/csc/).

If we were to boil all of that experience into a short piece of advice, it would be this: Be afraid of real dangers, but not of fabricated dangers. The Dover school board, who sought to require mention of ID in the biology classroom, was provided compelling evidence that their approach would lead them right off a cliff, yet they ignored the friendly advice urging them to take another approach. Here, fear could have served a useful function. In Ohio the school board members should not have allowed themselves to be frightened into opposing the strengths-and-weaknesses policy. The vast majority of Ohio citizens, from both parties, supported the strengths-and-weaknesses approach,[15] and it's never run into a lick of legal trouble.

To courage and prudence add commitment. Care more about protecting our kids from the one-sided, taxpayer-funded, Darwin-only propaganda of the methodological atheists than the methodological atheists care about recruiting your kids to their position. If there's a seemingly dull state school board election on the horizon, find out where the candidates stand on how Darwinism should be taught in the public schools. Finally, show up at the voting booth on election day, even when it's an off-year election, and even if it's "just a primary."

Be Ready to Give an Answer

One final thing to do to open minds to the evidence for intelligent design is to provide yourself the materials to be an effective advocate for intelligent design and academic freedom. This book is a starting point. The following list points to additional material, much of it available on the Internet, including advice on how to follow up when someone offers favorite comebacks to the main arguments for intelligent design. You can access these webpages either by typing the title and author into a search engine such as Google, or by using the URL available in the endnote.

- "Five Questions Evolutionists Would Rather Dodge" by William Dembski.[16]

- "Ten Questions to Ask Your Biology Teacher About Evolution" by Jonathan Wells.[17] See also his excellent follow-up piece, "Inherit the Spin: The National Center for Science Education Answers 'Ten Questions To Ask Your Biology Teacher About Evolution' with Evasions and Falsehoods."[18]

- "Ten Questions to Ask Your Biology Teacher About Design" by William Dembski.[19]

- "Top Questions and Answers About Intelligent Design Theory" by the Discovery Institute.[20]

- "Design and Darwinism," *Wittingshire's Bag End*. This website contains easy-to-read responses by Jonathan Witt and others, organized around a series of key questions, including "What Is Intelligent Design?" "Who Sees Evidence of Design?" "Who Sees Holes in Darwinism?" and "Is Intelligent Design a Christian Conspiracy?"[21]

- *The Design Revolution: Answering the Toughest Questions About Intelligent Design* by William Dembski, a book that provides a readable review of the various questions and objections Dembski has encountered in the many talks and debates he has been involved in at universities around the world during the past several years.[22]

- A one-stop portal into all things ID is located at <www.intelligentdesign.org>.

UNCENSORING DESIGN

This book began with a question: Are the things of nature the product of mindless forces alone, or did creative reason play a role? The question is fundamental because so much hinges on it. Are humans worthy of dignity? Are they endowed with certain unalienable rights? If humans are the mindless accident of blind nature, entering and exiting the cosmic stage without audience, in a universe without plan or purpose, what right do we have to puff ourselves up and talk of human rights and human dignity, of meaning or value or love? In such a cosmos, love is but a function of the glands, honor and loyalty nothing more than instincts programmed into us by a blind process of random genetic variation and natural selection. Such a cosmos is ultimately meaningless, a chasing after the wind.

At the heart of this book is a conviction rooted in reason and evidence: the evidence of nature points away from such a pointless universe and toward a universe charged with the grandeur of a design most remarkable. The book of nature tells us many stories. Some of those stories are mysterious, such as the stories of suffering and death in the natural world. The Jew and the Christian would say that it's through God's book of special revelation, the Bible, that we begin to understand such difficult mysteries. But as we have seen in these pages, the book of nature also tells a story of intelligent design, of a world charged with the evidence of a designing genius of unparalleled skill and power. That story matters because a culture's origin stories shape the fortunes of humans and nations, raising them up or casting them down to destruction.

The theory of intelligent design is first and foremost a scientific enterprise, but precisely because it considers the evidence for design in nature with objectivity and rigor, it has the power to help draw parts of our culture out of the wilderness of unmeaning. But to do this, certain chapters from the book of nature must be opened, not once, but again and again, and not by the one or the few, but by the many. The proponents of methodological atheism have for too long succeeded in censoring these chapters. It's time to lift the ban and shine a light.

Here is work.

Notes

Chapter 1: Fantastic Voyage
[1]The details of this voyage were inspired by Michael Denton's description of the cell in *Evolution: A Theory in Crisis* (Chevy Chase, Md.: Adler & Adler, 1986), pp. 328-30. The discussion of molecular machines draws from Michael Behe, *Darwin's Black Box: The Biochemical Challenge to Evolution*, rev. ed. (New York: Free Press, 2006), pp. 4-5.

Chapter 2: The Design Revolution
[1]Alfred Lord Tennyson, *In Memoriam A.H.H.* (1849), 56.15.

[2]Richard Dawkins, *The Blind Watchmaker* (New York: Norton, 1986), p. 6.

[3]Daniel C. Dennett, *Darwin's Dangerous Idea* (New York: Simon & Schuster, 1996), p. 63.

[4]Peter Slevin, "Battle on Teaching Evolution Sharpens," *Washington Post*, March 14, 2005, p. A1.

[5]See "Peer-Reviewed & Peer-Edited Scientific Publications Supporting the Theory of Intelligent Design (Annotated)," *Center for Science & Culture*, August 26, 2009 <www.discovery.org/a/2640>.

[6]Criticism of intelligent design in the mainstream biological literature is now so extensive that we give only a few examples: R. H. Thornhill and D. W. Ussery, "A Classification of Possible Routes of Darwinian Evolution," *Journal of Theoretical Biology* 203 (2000): 111-16. This paper presents a conceptual analysis of Michael Behe's claim that irreducible complexity poses an obstacle to Darwinian evolution. Thomas D. Schneider, "Evolution of Biological Information," *Nucleic Acids Research* 28, no. 14 (2000): 2794-799; and Richard E. Lenski, Charles Ofria, Robert T. Pennock and Christoph Adami, "The Evolutionary Origin of Complex Features," *Nature* 423 (2003): 139-44. These last two papers offer computational simulations that are supposed to demonstrate Darwinian evolutionary pathways leading to irreducible complexity. Reviews of intelligent design books are also increasingly common in the biological

literature. For instance, William Dembski's *No Free Lunch* was reviewed by Brian Charlesworth in "Evolution by Design?" *Nature* 418 (2002): 129.

[7]Eugenie Scott, "'Science and Religion,' 'Christian Scholarship,' and 'Theistic Science': Some Comparisons," *Reports of the National Center for Science Education* 18, no. 2 (1998): 30-32. A version that might be slightly different is available online at <http://ncseweb.org/rncse/18/2/science-religion-christian-scholarship-theistic-science>.

[8]Nicolaus Copernicus, *On the Revolutions of the Heavenly Spheres*, preface and book I, trans. by John F. Dobson and Selig Brodetsky, in *Theories of the Universe: From Babylonian Myth to Modern Science*, ed. Milton K. Munitz (New York: Simon & Schuster, 1965), pp. 149-73.

[9]Arno Penzias, "Creation Is Supported by All the Data So Far," *Cosmos, Bios, and Theos*, ed. H. Margenau and R. A. Varghese (La Salle, Ill.: Open Court, 1992), p. 83.

[10]See Guillermo Gonzalez and Jay W. Richards, *The Privileged Planet* (Washington, D.C.: Regnery, 2004); William Lane Craig, *Theism, Atheism, and Big Bang Cosmology* (New York: Oxford University Press, 1993); and Stephen C. Meyer, "Evidence for Design in Physics and Biology: From the Origin of the Universe to the Origin of Life," in *Science and Evidence for Design in the Universe* (San Francisco: Ignatius Press, 2000), pp. 53-111.

[11]Various philosophers have discussed the analogy, including John Leslie and Richard Swinburne. See John Leslie, *Universes* (London: Routledge, 1989), pp. 13-15, 108, 125, 148-49, 158, 161.

[12]Thomas Kuhn, *The Structure of Scientific Revolutions*, 2nd ed. (Chicago: University of Chicago Press, 1970).

[13]For the current view, see Philip Kearey and Frederick J. Vine, *Global Tectonics* (Oxford: Blackwell Sciences, 1996). For the former view, known as the geosynclinal theory, which was subsequently discarded, see Thomas H. Clark and Colin W. Stearn, *The Geological Evolution of North America* (New York: Ronald Press, 1960). Clark and Stearn remark, "The geosynclinal theory is one of the great unifying principles in geology. In many ways its role in geology is similar to that of the theory of evolution, which serves to integrate the many branches of the biological sciences. . . . Just as the doctrine of evolution is universally accepted among biologists, so also the geosynclinal origin of the major mountain

systems is an established principle in geology" (p. 43). The geosynclinal theory is now dead and buried.

[14]Michael Crichton, "Aliens Cause Global Warming," speech delivered at the California Institute of Technology, Pasadena, California, January 17, 2003, available at <www.michaelcrichton.net/speech-alienscauseglobal warming.html>.

[15]The title of an article at BNET on the poll of physicians, "Majority of Physicians Give the Nod to Evolution Over Intelligent Design" <http://findarticles.com/p/articles/mi_m0EIN/is_2005_May_23/ai_n13774053> is somewhat misleading. By comparing the results of Q6 to Q7 of the poll, it's clear that many doctors considered intelligently guided evolution to be in the "evolution" category rather than in the "intelligent design" category. Only with Q7, where unguided models of evolution (like Darwinism) are teased apart from intelligently guided evolution, does it become clear that a distinct majority of U.S. physicians doubt Darwinism and see intelligent design playing a role in the origin of humans.

[16]Stephen Jay Gould, *Ever Since Darwin: Reflections in Natural History* (New York: W. W. Norton, 1977), p. 267.

[17]Peter Singer, *A Darwinian Left: Politics, Evolution, and Cooperation* (New Haven, Conn.: Yale University Press, 2000), p. 6.

[18]Compare Dembski's explicitly theological book *Intelligent Design: The Bridge Between Science and Theology* (Downers Grove, Ill.: InterVarsity Press, 1999) with his peer-reviewed research monograph *The Design Inference: Eliminating Chance Through Small Probabilities* (Cambridge: Cambridge University Press, 1998), which appeared in *Cambridge Studies in Probability, Induction, and Decision Theory*.

[19]Francis Crick and Leslie E. Orgel, "Directed Panspermia," *Icarus* 19 (1973): 341-46.

[20]Eliot Marshall, "Medline Searches Turn Up Cases of Suspected Plagiarism," *Science* 279 (1998): 473-74.

[21]Nathaniel Hawthorne, *The Complete Novels and Selected Tales of Nathaniel Hawthorne*, ed. N. H. Pearson (New York: Random House, 1937), p. 1171.

[22]Dawkins, *Blind Watchmaker*, p. 1.

[23]Francis Crick, *What Mad Pursuit: A Personal View of Scientific Discovery* (New York: Basic Books, 1988), p. 138.

Chapter 3: The World's Smallest Rotary Engine

[1]See Kenneth Miller, "The Flagellum Unspun: The Collapse of 'Irreducible Complexity,'" in *Debating Design: From Darwin to DNA*, ed. William Dembski and Michael Ruse (Cambridge: Cambridge University Press, 2004), pp. 81-97. The article is also available at Miller's personal website <www.millerandlevine.com/km/evol/design2/article.html>.

[2]For more on Lyell and his criterion of "causes now in operation," see Stephen C. Meyer, "A Scientific History—and Philosophical Defense—of the Theory of Intelligent Design," in *Religion, Staat, Gesellschaft* 7, no. 2 (2006): 12-14. The article is available at The Center for Science & Culture's website <www.discovery.org/a/7471>.

[3]Behe responds to Miller's critique of his irreducible complexity argument, "Irreducible Complexity: Obstacle to Darwinian Evolution," in *Debating Design*, pp. 352-70, and in the afterword of the tenth anniversary edition of *Darwin's Black Box* (New York: Simon & Schuster, 2006).

[4]Kenneth R. Miller, "Answering the Biochemical Argument from Design," in *God and Design: The Teleological Argument and Modern Science*, ed. Neil Manson (New York: Routledge, 2003). A prepublication version of the article is available at Miller's website <www.millerandlevine.com/km/evol/design1/article.html>.

[5]Mike Gene, "Evolving the Bacterial Flagellum Through Mutation and Cooption," *Teleologic* <http://webarchive.org/web/20080618180140/http://www.idthink.net/biot/flag1/index.html>.

[6]"Gram-Negative Bacteria Shoot Their Way into Cells," *Biology News Net*, June 1, 2005 <www.biologynews.net/archives/2005/06/01/gram negative_bacteria_shoot_their_way_into_cells.html>.

[7]Scott A. Minnich and Stephen C. Meyer, "Genetic Analysis of Coordinate Flagellar and Type III Regulatory Circuits in Pathogenic Bacteria," in *Design in Nature II: Comparing Design in Nature with Science and Engineering* (Southampton, U.K.: WIT Press, 2004). This article is available online at the Discovery Institute's website <www.discovery.org/scripts/viewDB/filesDB-download.php?id=389>. Thanks to Casey Luskin for providing a helpful preliminary response to Miller's paper. The analysis is also indebted to Michael Behe, John Bracht and Mike Gene for their insights. Following are sources used in the discussion of the bacterial flagellum: S.-I. Aizawa, "Flagellar Assembly in Salmonella Typhimurium," *Molecular Microbiology* 19 (1996): 1-5; and S.-I. Aizawa, "Bacte-

rial Flagella and Biological Design," 2001 <http://iscid.org/papers/ Bracht_InventionsAlgorithms_112601.pdf>; J. R. Bracht, "The Bacterial Flagellum: A Response to Ursula Goodenough," 2002 <http://iscid.org/ papers/Bracht_GoodenoughResponse_021203.pdf>; Richard Dawkins, *The Blind Watchmaker* (New York: Norton, 1986); William Dembski, "ID as a Theory of Technological Evolution," August 10, 2001 <http:// iscid.org/papers/Dembski_TechnologicalEvolution_120901 .pdf>; William Dembski, *No Free Lunch: Why Specified Complexity Cannot Be Purchased Without Intelligence* (Lanham, Md.: Rowman & Littlefield, 2002); Mike Gene, "Evolving the Bacterial Flagellum Through Mutation and Cooption" <http://web.archive.org/web/20080618180140/ http://www.idthink.net/biot/flag1/index.html>; Franklin Harold, *The Way of the Cell: Molecules, Organisms and the Order of Life* (New York: Oxford University Press, 2001); C. J. Hueck, "Type III Protein Secretion Systems in Bacterial Pathogens of Animals and Plants," *Microbiology and Molecular Biology Reviews* 62 (1998): 379-433; Kenneth Miller, *Finding Darwin's God: A Scientist's Search for Common Ground Between God and Evolution* (New York: HarperCollins, 1999); L. Nguyen et al., "Phylogenetic Analyses of the Constituents of Type III Protein Secretion Systems," *Journal of Molecular Microbiology Biotechnology* 2, no. 2 (2000): 125-44; S. D. Savransky, *Engineering of Creativity: Introduction to TRIZ Methodology of Inventive Problem Solving* (Boca Raton, Fla.: CRC Press, 2000); T. D. Schneider, "Evolution of Biological Information," *Nucleic Acids Research* 28, no. 14 (2000): 2794-799; S.-I. Aizawa, "Bacterial Flagella and Type III Secretion Systems," *FEMS Microbiology Letters* 202 (2001): 157-64; Michael Behe, *Darwin's Black Box* (New York: Free Press, 1996); Michael Behe, "Irreducible Complexity: Obstacle to Darwinian Evolution," in *Debating Design: From Darwin to DNA*, ed. William A. Dembski and Michael Ruse (Cambridge: Cambridge University Press, 2004); J. R. Bracht, "Inventions, Algorithms, and Biological Design" <www.iscid .org/papers/Bracht_InventionsAlgorithms_112601.pdf>.

[8]See Nguyen et al., "Phylogenetic Analyses," and Scott A. Minnich and Stephen C. Meyer, "Genetic Analysis of Coordinate Flagellar and Type III Regulatory Circuits in Pathogenic Bacteria," in *Design and Nature II: Proceedings of the Second International Conference on Design & Nature*, ed. M. W. Collins and C. A. Brebbia (Southampton, U.K.: WIT Press, 2004).

[9]Theodosius Dobzhansky, "Biology, Molecular and Organismic," *American Zoologist* 4, no. 4 (1964): 443-52.

[10]"Claim CB200.1," *Talk.Origins* <www.talkorigins.org/indexcc/CBCB200_1.html>.

[11]See Michael Behe, "The Lamest Attempt Yet to Answer the Challenge Irreducible Complexity Poses for Darwinian Evolution," *Intelligent Design the Future*, April 6, 2006 <www.idthefuture.com/2006/04/the_lamest_attempt_yet_to_answ.html>, a response to an article in the journal *Science,* which purported to provide laboratory evidence against Behe's irreducible complexity argument.

[12]Casey Luskin, "When the Mona Lisa Appears on a Hillside, Do You Infer Intelligent Design?" *Evolution News and Views* 8, no. 16 (2006) <www.evolutionnews.org/2006/08/when_the_mona_lisa_appears_on.html>.

[13]Franklin Harold, *The Way of the Cell* (New York: Oxford University Press, 2001), p. 205.

[14]The World Skeptics Conference was organized by CSICOP and held in summer 2002. For a summary of the conference, see Kendrick Frazier and Ben Radford, "Fourth World Skeptics Conference in Burbank a Lively Foment of Ideas," *Skeptical Inquirer* 26, no. 5 (September/October 2002), available at <www.csicop.org/si/show/fourth_world_skeptics_conference_in_burbank_a_lively_foment_of_ideas/>.

Chapter 4: The Design Test

[1]In the 1940s Claude Shannon of Bell Laboratories developed a theory of information in which he determined the amount of possible information in a sequence of characters by calculating how improbable the arrangement of characters was. See Claude Shannon, "A Mathematical Theory of Communication," *Bell System Technical Journal* 27 (1948): 379-423, 623-56. The more improbable (or complex) the arrangement, the more Shannon information, or information carrying capacity, a string or system possesses.

[2]To begin to answer this question, we first have to understand what we want our design detection test to do reliably. Every test created by humans has its limitations. Think of medical tests. By coming up positive a medical test is supposed to indicate the presence of a disease, and by coming up negative it's supposed to indicate the absence of the disease. A

perfectly reliable medical test would detect the presence of a disease whenever it's really present and never detect it whenever it's absent. Unfortunately, no medical test is perfectly reliable. A false positive occurs when the test says that a well person is sick, and a false negative occurs when the test says a sick person is well. In building a medical test for a disease, doctors try to keep the number of false positives and false negatives as low as possible. Now all human tests, not just medical tests, face the problem of false positives and false negatives. But in many cases, one can weight the test to avoid one or the other. If you want to avoid weeding out people who might turn out to be good doctors (false negatives), don't make your medical exams overly difficult. On the other hand, if you mainly want to avoid giving medical degrees to doctors who are undertrained or insufficiently talented (false positives), make the medical exams extremely difficult. In trying to construct a good design test, which is more important, avoiding false negatives or avoiding false positives? For the theory of intelligent design, the answer is clear. If our design test says something in nature is designed, we want to have confidence in that finding. We want to avoid false positives, even if that means constructing a test that sometimes misses things that were designed. For the statistics behind medical tests, see Charles H. Hennekens and Julie E. Buring, *Epidemiology in Medicine* (Boston: Little, Brown, 1987), chap. 13.

[3]See Stuart Kauffman, *Investigations* (New York: Oxford University Press, 2000); Emile Borel, *Probabilities and Life*, trans. M. Baudin (New York: Dover, 1962), p. 28. Kenneth Dam and Herbert Lin, *Cryptography's Role in Securing the Information Society* (Washington, D.C.: National Academies Press, 1996); Seth Lloyd, letters, *Physical Review*, June 10, 2002.

[4]Michael Denton, *Evolution: A Theory in Crisis* (Chevy Chase, Md.: Adler & Adler, 1986), p. 250.

[5]See Stephen Meyer, "DNA and the Origin of Life: Information, Specification, and Explanation," in *Darwinism, Design, and Public Education*, ed. John Angus Campbell and Stephen C. Meyer (East Lansing: Michigan State University Press, 2003), pp. 223-85. The essay engages the ongoing conversation among molecular biologists and information theorists, drawing on works too numerous to list here. A few that are particularly relevant to this aspect of his discussion are J. Reidhaar-Olson and R. Sauer, "Functionally Acceptable Solutions in Two Alpha-

Helical Regions of Lambda Repressor," *Proteins, Structure, Function, and Genetics* 7 (1990): 306-10; D. D. Axe, "Biological Function Places Unexpectedly Tight Constraints on Protein Sequences," *Journal of Molecular Biology* 301, no. 3 (2000): 585-96; M. Behe, "Experimental Support for Regarding Functional Classes of Proteins to Be Highly Isolated from Each Other," in *Darwinism: Science or Philosophy?* ed. J. Buell and V. Hearn (Richardson, Tex.: Foundation for Thought and Ethics, 1994), pp. 60-71; H. P. Yockey, *Information Theory and Molecular Biology* (Cambridge: Cambridge University Press, 1992), pp. 246-58; E. Pennisi, "Seeking Life's Bare Genetic Necessities," *Science* 272 (1996): 1098-99; A. Mushegian and E. Koonin, "A Minimal Gene Set for Cellular Life Derived by Comparison of Complete Bacterial Genomes," *Proceedings of the National Academy of Sciences* 93 (1996): 10268-273; and C. Bult et al., "Complete Genome Sequence of the Methanogenic Archaeon, *Methanococcus Jannasch*," *Science* 273 (1996): 1058-72.

[6]William Dembski, *The Design Revolution* (Downers Grove, Ill.: InterVarsity Press, 2004).

[7]Antony Flew, "Interview with Gary Habermas," *Philosophia Christi* 6, no. 2 (2004) <www.biola.edu/antonyflew>.

[8]Michael J. Behe, *The Edge of Evolution: The Search for the Limits of Darwinism* (New York: Free Press, 2007), pp. 15-16. The book has attracted published critical reviews from several leading evolutionists. Behe summarizes and responds to their various objections at <http://behe.uncommondescent.com/>, primarily in the 2007 portion of the archives.

[9]See the sidebar in section 1.3 of William Dembski and Jonathan Wells's *The Design of Life: Discovering Signs of Intelligence in Biological Systems* (Richardson, Tex.: Foundation for Thought and Ethics, 2007). These differences between humans and chimps are taken from a much longer list by Geoffrey Simmons, *What Darwin Didn't Know* (Eugene, Ore.: Harvest House, 2004), pp. 274-78.

[10]Jonathan Wells, *Icons of Evolution* (Washington, D.C.: Regnery, 2000); and "Critics Rave Over Icons of Evolution: A Response to Published Reviews," *Center for Science & Culture*, June 12, 2002 <www.discovery.org/a/1180>.

[11]Much of the material on the GULO pseudogene is adopted from Dembski and Wells, *Design of Life*, sec. 5.6.

[12]Jonathan Wells summarizes his hypothesis and explains the design rea-

soning that led to it in "Using Intelligent Design Theory to Guide Scientific Research," *PCID* 3, no. 1.2 (2004) <www.iscid.org/papers/Wells_TOPS_051304.pdf>. He lays out the hypothesis in greater detail in "Do Centrioles Generate a Polar Ejection Force," *Rivista di Biologia/Biology Forum* 98 (2005): 37-62 <www.discovery.org/a/2680>.

[13]Bill Gates, *The Road Ahead* (New York: Viking, 1995), p. 188.

[14]William A. Dembski and Robert J. Marks II, "Conservation of Information in Search: Measuring the Cost of Success," *IEEE Transactions on Systems, Man and Cybernetics A, Systems & Humans* 5, no. 5 (September 2009): 1051-61. For this paper and the other work of the lab, see <www.EvoInfo.org>.

[15]Philip S. Skell, "Why Do We Invoke Darwin," *The Scientist* 19, no. 16 (2005): 10.

Chapter 5: The Poison of Materialism

[1]Daniel Patrick Moynihan, *American Educator* 17, no. 4 (1993-1994): 10-18.

[2]Clarence Darrow, "Speech of Clarence Darrow," in *The Loeb-Leopold Case*, ed. Alvin V. Sellars (Brunswick, Ga.: Classic Publishing, 1926), pp. 168-69; see also John West, *Darwin Day in America: How Our Politics and Culture Have Been Dehumanized in the Name of Science* (Wilmington, Del.: ISI Books, 2007), pp. 45-49.

[3]Oliver Wendell Holmes, quoted in Albert W. Alschuler, *Law Without Values: The Life, Work, and Legacy of Justice Holmes* (Chicago: University of Chicago Press, 2000), p. 28.

[4]Oliver Wendell Holmes, "Buck vs. Bell," Cornell University Law School: Supreme Court Collection <www.law.cornell.edu/supct/html/historics/USSC_CR_0274_0200_ZO.html>.

[5]For details about the Buck case and more on the history of sterilization and eugenics in the United States, see West, "Breeding Our Way out of Poverty," in *Darwin Day in America*.

[6]Mark Haller, *Eugenics: Hereditarian Attitudes in American Thought* (New Brunswick, N.J.: Rutgers University Press, 1963), p. 141.

[7]Charles Darwin, *The Descent of Man*, 2nd ed. (1874), chap. 5 <www.gutenberg.org/dirs/etext00/dscmn10.txt>.

[8]For a fuller discussion of Darwin's views on natural selection as applied to humans, see West, *Darwin Day in America*, pp. 31-34.

[9]Daniel C. Dennett, *Darwin's Dangerous Idea: Evolution and the Meanings of Life* (New York: Simon & Schuster, 1996), p. 63.

[10]Edward O. Wilson, *On Human Nature* (Cambridge, Mass.: Harvard University Press, 1978), pp. 195, 204.

[11]T. S. Eliot, "The Wasteland," ll. 19-24, *Bartleby.com* <www.bartleby.com/201/1.html>.

[12]Charles Darwin, letter to William Graham, July 3, 1881, Darwin Correspondence Project <www.darwinproject.ac.uk/darwinletters/calendar/entry-13230.html>.

[13]Darwin, *Descent of Man*, chap. 6 <www.gutenberg.org/dirs/etext00/dscmn10.txt>.

[14]Charles Darwin, *Origin of Species* (London: John Murray, 1859), chaps. 7, 14 <www.gutenberg.org/dirs/etext98/otoos11.txt>.

[15]Richard Weikart, *From Darwin to Hitler: Evolutionary Ethics, Eugenics, and Racism in Germany* (New York: Palgrave Macmillan, 2006), p. 233.

[16]Edward T. Oakes, "Darwin's Graveyards," *Books & Culture*, November-December 2006 <www.christianitytoday.com/bc/2006/novdec/15.35.html>.

Chapter 6: Breaking the Spell of Materialism

[1]See Howard J. van Till, "The Fully Gifted Creation," in *Three Views of Creation and Evolution*, ed. J. P. Moreland and John Mark Reynolds (Grand Rapids: Zondervan, 1999), pp. 159-218.

[2]This quotation, spoken by Paul in Acts 17:28, is from a Greek poem attributed to Epimenides the Cretan.

[3]Steve Mirsky, "Sticker Shock," *Scientific American*, February 2005.

[4]The description of Kierkegaard is taken from Jonah Avriel Cohen, "Why Intelligent Design Theory Ought to Be Taught," *The American Thinker*, August 25, 2005 <www.americanthinker.com/2005/08/why_intelligent_design_theory.html>.

[5]Paul Thomas, letter to *Touchstone* magazine emailed July 5, 2004, responding to Witt's July/August 2004 *Touchstone* essay, "The Gods Must Be Tidy." Witt quoted from, and responded to, the letter in "Nature's Book Shelved," March 2006, available at <www.touchstonemag.com/archives/author.php?id=188>.

[6]Antony Flew, "Interview with Gary Habermas," *Philosophia Christi*, winter 2004 <www.biola.edu/antonyflew>.

[7]Søren Kierkegaard, *Philosophical Fragments*, trans. David F. Swenson, 2nd ed., trans. Howard V. Hong (Princeton, N.J.: Princeton University

Press, 1962), p. 52. In the same book, commentator Niels Thulstrup points to the probable source of Kierkegaard's argument, earlier writings by G. E. Lessing and D. F. Strauss.

[8]See William Paley, "The Goodness of the Deity," in *Natural Theology* (Lancaster, Penn.: Coachwhip, 2005), pp. 252-91.

[9]See William Dembski, *The Design Inference: Eliminating Chance Through Small Probabilities* (Cambridge: Cambridge University Press, 1998).

Chapter 7: The Book of Nature

[1]Daniel C. Dennett, *Darwin's Dangerous Idea* (New York: Simon & Schuster, 1996), p. 63.

[2]Barbara Bradley Hagerty, "Intelligent Design and Academic Freedom," National Public Radio, November 10, 2005 <www.npr.org/templates/story/story.php?storyId=5007508>.

[3]For a roundup of attacks, see Austin Cline, "Outing Barbara Bradley Hagerty," *Austin's Atheism Blog*, May 21, 2004 <http://atheism.about.com/b/2004/05/21/outing-barbara-bradley-hagerty.htm>.

[4]P. Z. Myers, "A New Recruit," *Panda's Thumb*, June 13, 2005 <http://pandasthumb.org/archives/2005/06/a-new-recruit.html#c35130>. The statement is made in Myers's follow-up comment on June 14, 2005 <http://pandasthumb.org/archives/2005/06/a-new-recruit.html#comment-panels>.

[5]Liz Craig, Kansas City for Science Discussion Forums, February 10, 2005 <www.kcfs.org/cgibin/ultimatebb.cgi?ubb=get_topic;f=3;t=000017>. This URL is no longer valid, but Craig's statement is now available at <www.kansasscience2005.com/To%20whom%20this%20may%20concern.pdf>. Craig's comment goes some way toward explaining why many reporters thought the Kansas science standards at that time called for the teaching of intelligent design (they didn't), and why they thought they'd changed the standard definition of science (they didn't; instead, they brought the definition back into line with the most common definition among state science standards).

[6]Phillip Johnson, *Reason in the Balance: The Case Against Naturalism in Science, Law and Education* (Downers Grove, Ill.: InterVarsity Press, 1995), p. 216.

[7]See the November 19, 2004, Gallup Poll "Third of Americans Say Evidence Has Supported Darwin's Evolution Theory" <www.gallup.com/

poll/14107/Third-Americans-Say-Evidence-Has-Supported-Darwins
-Evolution-Theory.aspx>. The title is misleading since the figure combines
evolution guided by intelligent design with purely Darwinian evolution.

[8]Sophia Maines, "Second KU Class Denies Status of Science to Design
Theory," LJWorld.com, November 27, 2005 <www2.ljworld.com/
news/2005/nov/27/2nd_ku_class_denies_status_science_design_
theory/?city_local>.

[9]For a full discussion of the doctor's poll, including a link to the poll and
to an organization of doctors skeptical of Darwinism, see Jonathan
Witt's post at *Evolution News & Views*, May 4, 2006 <www.evolution
news.org/2006/05/new_darwin_dissent_list_for_th.html>.

[10]After a U.S. Justice Department investigation was launched, Dini agreed
to alter his policy and the Justice Department investigation was dropped.
The new policy asked for students seeking a recommendation to demonstrate an ability to explain the theory of evolution. See Larry Taylor, "Biology Professor Alters Evolution Statement for Recommendations; Justice Ends Probe," *BNET Business Network* <http://web.archive.org/
web/20080625055536re_/findarticles.com/p/articles/mi_m2843/
is_4_27/ai_1047332>, adopted from the original article in July-August
issue of *Skeptical Inquirer*. This is an improvement brought about
through publicity and public pressure. However, it's important to recognize the limited nature of the victory. Imagine an excellent student in
Dini's class, with top grades and demonstrated talent for experimental
biology went to Professor Dini and asked for a recommendation to medical school. The professor asks the student to explain the theory of evolution. Other students had obtained a recommendation after regurgitating
the main talking points in favor of modern evolutionary theory. But this
student goes one step further. She offers a robust description of the evidence both for and against the theory of evolution, evidence she cor-
roborates with ample citations from the peer-reviewed biological literature. Would the student leave the office with a recommendation in hand?
Neither of us is optimistic about such a prospect. To understand why,
see Dini's letter to the editor of the *Skeptical Inquirer*, where he defended
the original policy. The letter appeared in the November-December
2003 (vol. 27.6) issue.

[11]For an in-depth response to the Judge Jones opinion, see David DeWolf
et al., *Traipsing into Evolution: Intelligent Design and the Kitzmiller vs.*

Dover Decision (Seattle: Discovery Institute Press, 2006). For pro-and-con law review articles, see the winter 2007 issue of *Montana Law Review*. The first article, "Intelligent Design Will Survive Kitzmiller v. Dover," is written by David DeWolf, John West and Casey Luskin. The second article, "Disaster in Dover" by Peter Irons, responds to the first article, followed by a brief rebuttal to Irons from DeWolf, West and Luskin. All three are available online at <www.discovery.org/a/3877>.

[12]Amy Worden, "Bad Frog Beer to 'Intelligent Design,'" *Philadelphia Inquirer*, October 16, 2005 <www.thefire.org/pdfs/06cf275fc2c90c9a80a f51a1f35c33b5.pdf>.

[13]Edward J. Larson, *Summer for the Gods* (New York: Basic Books, 1997).

[14]For an extensive list see "Peer-Reviewed & Peer-Edited Scientific Publications Supporting the Theory of Intelligent Design," *Center for Science & Culture*, August 26, 2009 <www.discovery.org/a/2640>.

[15]"Results from Nationwide Poll," *Zogby International*, March 6, 2006 <www.discovery.org/scripts/viewDB/filesDB-download.php?command =download&id=719>. By a more than three-to-one margin to those who opposed the idea, polled voters said biology teachers should teach Darwin's theory of evolution, but also the scientific evidence against it. Approximately seven in ten (69 percent) sided with this view. In contrast, only about one in five (21 percent) felt that biology teachers should teach only Darwin's theory of evolution and the scientific evidence that supports it. Not only do a majority of people in virtually every subgroup agree that the evidence both for and against should be presented when teaching evolution, but people in every subgroup are at least twice as likely to prefer this approach to science education. Among the biggest supporters are 18-29 year-olds (88 percent). Others who strongly support this approach include 69 percent of African Americans, 70 percent of 35-54 year-olds and 60 percent of Democrats.

[16]William Dembski, "Five Questions," *DesignInference.com* <www .designinference.com/documents/2004.04.Five_Questions_Ev.pdf>.

[17]Jonathan Wells, "Ten Questions to Ask Your Biology Teacher About Evolution," *Icons of Evolution* <www.iconsofevolution.com/tools/questions .php3>.

[18]Jonathan Wells, "Inherit the Spin," Center for Science & Culture, January 15, 2002 <www.discovery.org/a/1106>.

[19]William Dembski, "Ten Questions," DesignInference.com <www.designinference.com/documents/2004.01.Ten_Questions_ID.pdf>.

[20]"Top Questions and Answers About Intelligent Design," Center for Science & Culture, September 8, 2005 <www.discovery.org/a/2348>.

[21]Jonathan Witt, "Design and Darwinism," *Wittingshire's Bag End* <http://wittingshirebagend.blogspot.com/2005/02/design-and-darwinism.html>.

[22]William Dembski, *The Design Revolution* (Downers Grove, Ill.: InterVarsity Press, 2004). See <www.amazon.com/Design-Revolution-Answering-Questions-Intelligent/dp/0830823751>.

Index

(Note: Italicized page numbers denote an illustration.)